She Built Ships During WW II

Historical Fiction

We Can Do it!

Jeane Slone

Jeane Slone

PRAISE FOR *She Built Ships During WW II:*

With meticulous research on the WW II era, Slone weaves an intricate story of cruelty, compassion, and love, reminding us of the injustice of the internment of Japanese-Americans and racial prejudice in the Armed Forces. The courage of women welders who built ships while their husbands were at war is depicted so well that the characters come to life. We watch the heroine, Lolly, struggle to keep her family together while she works as a welder while her husband is away. A tender romance is threaded throughout the book and we agonize with her as she brings it to an inevitable conclusion. Between the fascinating and sometimes little-known historical facts, and the larger than life sympathetic characters, the book is a page-turner to the very end.
— Alla Crone, author of *Rodina* and *The Other Side of Life.*

Cover your eyes! I have a flash for you. Jeane Slone has written another World War II historical fiction that will make you blink. *She Built Ships During WW II,* is a novel about Lolly, a housewife who became a skilled welder in a naval shipyard. Ms. Slone weaves a story of the difficulty about keeping home and hearth whole while fighting the prejudices of the era and changing women's roles in American society. Slone's historical fiction reveals many of America's painful moments during a tragic time and continues her own mission of giving women their rightful place in the victory in World War II.
— Michael D. Mullins, Vice President, Military Writers Society of America. Author of *Vietnam in Verse.*

The details that Jeane Slone fills this well-researched novel with make the pages of *She Built Ships During World War II,* come alive. It's the 1940s and Uncle Sam collects silk stockings for gunpowder bags, Victory Visitors knock on the door, food is rationed and husbands leave home. Lolly corresponds with her friend, Sumi, who has gone from running the community market to a Japanese-American Internment Camp at the San Bruno racetrack. Sumi is pregnant. Lolly's husband enlists in the Navy and now both Joe and Lolly will see their lives take unexpected curves. Hattie works with Lolly building ships. She is colored and her husband, who is a Tuskegee Airman, and finds himself in constant turmoil. Share these women's struggles, how they manage their children, jobs, their loves, and the fleeting joys, they find in these difficult times.

— Linda Loveland Reid, President Redwood Writer's Club, Santa Rosa. Author of *Touch of Magenta.*

SHE BUILT SHIPS DURING WORLD WAR II
Copyright 2012 Jeane Slone/Walter J. Willey Book Company

ISBN 978-0-9838154-1-9
Library of Congress Control Number 2012904709

Printed in the United State of America

Cover Design: Jelehla Ziemba/Word Art: JZ@ZWordArt.com

Front Cover: Wendy the Welder, Dorothy Price, Runner-up, "Joan of Arc" welding contest, Richmond Kaiser Shipyard #3, July, 1943. Permission from The Richmond Museum of History, Richmond, CA.

Back Cover:
Black welder: 22-year-old Gladys Thews of Richmond, California, taken by Emmanuel Joseph, Franklin Delano Roosevelt Presidential Library collection.

Ink drawing of Mine Okubo from her book Citizen 13660, 1946, published by University of Washington Press with permission from her estate, Seiko Buckingham.

This novel is historically accurate. All the characters have been fictionalized.

Acknowledgments

I would like to thank the following people who helped make this historical fiction come to life.

My brother, Tom Slone, for all his photography research

My son, Glenn Kerbein, emergency computer technician

My husband, Dennis M. Ness, for his critical ear

My father-in-law, Dennis L. Ness, for technical advice on welding

Sivani Lloyd, true friend and avid reader

Kathleen Turner, assisting in research

Ranger Thaddeus Shay, for his informative tour of Port Chicago

Richmond Museum of History, Richmond, CA

Rosie the Riveter/WW II Home Front National Historical Park

U.C. Berkeley, research center

My editors, Stephanie Freele, and Cris Wanzer/Manuscripts to Go

All the members of Healdsburg Literary Guild, CA and Redwood Writers Club, CA

The tour of the *SS Red Oak* Victory Ship, Richmond, CA, and *S.S. Jeremiah O'Brien* Liberty Ship, San Francisco, CA

Rosie the Riveter Oral History website

Japanese-American National Museum in Los Angeles for its realistic hands on exhibit of the Japanese-American Internment

Benjamin Whitaker, welding teacher at Santa Rosa Junior College, Santa Rosa, CA

Densho: The Japanese-American Legacy Project, oral history web site, Tom Ikeda, Director

Arlene Miller, author, *The Best Little Grammar Book Ever*

All my children and my listening paddling buddies

Table of Contents

Introduction

Let us not forget the good parts of history, in order to enjoy them.

Let us not forget the bad parts of history, in order to not repeat them.

Chapter 1: The Only Japanese I Knew

Every night when Joe came home from his trucking job, he would ask me how my day went and if the children had done anything bad. I would only tell him if Billy acted up, then Joe would take him over his knee and give him a few smart swats. Edna rarely misbehaved, though her tattling got on my nerves.

One particular evening, I got the children to bed early so I could listen to the radio and knit more wool soakers for Billy. I never had enough soakers. Why, oh why couldn't he use the toilet like Edna? She had trained nice and young. I wished Mother was still alive, or at least my sister Diana nearby to talk to about my troubles. Sumi's son was already potty trained. She was such an intelligent, practical person, and I wanted to ask her how she had done it. I certainly couldn't discuss Billy and the pot with Joe. He would just give me a sideways look and mutter, "That's your problem, not mine."

Joe stomped in and unplugged the Zenith.

With a soft voice I protested, "Joe, I was listening to the Pepsodent show."

He was back in the garage before I could finish the sentence. I furiously clicked the knitting needles, tightly wrapping the grey yarn. Joe returned and plugged in a different radio.

"Much better." He grinned. "The Silvertone has a

wider range and finer quality to it."

"I think I'll go to Sumi's store tomorrow. The children love seeing her new Scottish terrier."

Joe squinted his eyes at me, causing his mustache to twitch. "Jeeesus, what kind of name is Sumi?"

"She's Japanese," I mumbled as he went back to his workshop in the garage. I felt uncomfortable whenever he used the Lord's name in vain.

I click, click, clicked away, listening to Bob Hope's wisecracking monologue. "Kids are wonderful, but I like mine barbecued," he quipped. I snickered, thinking he sure could be nasty!

In the morning, Edna rushed into the kitchen with her long, brown pigtails bouncing behind. "Billy keeps pinching me, make him stop!"

"Pinch him back, and leave me alone; I have to do the dishes."

I filled up the sink with the breakfast bowls.

"Can we go see Fala?" Billy asked, grabbing my legs.

"Only if you're nice to your sister." I bubbled the Ivory soap flakes in the Wheatena pot, and enjoyed the silky feel of them. I isolated one of the bubbles and blew it into the air, wishing I were wrapped up inside, floating away.

Billy skipped toward Edna yelling, "We get to see Fala and Frankie today!"

The lone bubble popped as I wiped my hands on my floral apron. In the cupboard, I shook the round oatmeal cardboard container. Upon hearing the rattle of only a few oats left, I got my pencil from on top of the Coldspot and wrote "oatmeal" on the back of a used, tattered envelope. I added a few more items on the list to bring to Matsumotos' grocery store.

Slipping into the bedroom, I held my mother's brush and stroked my plain, dark brown hair, enjoying the feel of the long, heavy, gold-laced handle. I couldn't do much about the ordinary color of my hair, but at least the waves gave it some personality. One more sweep of my hair, just like Mama used to do. Peering into the children's room, I smiled, watching them build blocks together without bickering.

"Come into the bathroom. I need to wash your faces, then we'll walk down to the store."

Edna dragged her brother into the bathroom while he swatted at her. I wiped Billy's cheeks until he protested, then washed Edna's just to be fair.

"Put your shoes on and help Billy with his. I'll fetch the grocery cart," I said to Edna.

"I get first ride," Billy said, jumping up and down on a handmade, worn braided rug in the hallway.

"You always get to be first." Edna's lips formed a pout. "Let me be first this time."

As they squabbled, I went to the hall closet for our coats, wishing they didn't have to argue about every little thing. At least the rain hadn't come, which made for a chilly November.

Exhausted by their fighting, I held the metal handle of the two-wheeled cart and put Billy inside just to keep him quiet. Edna whined with her unfair, sulking look.

The cool, breezy air of the small town of Richmond felt delightful. The children kept occupied as we walked. We watched an orange cat slip by, along with the occasional bird in the waving leaves of the walnut trees. When we reached the Matsumotos', I pulled the heavy store door, causing an ornate oriental bell to clang. I helped Billy scramble out of the tall, oblong cart.

Little Frankie ran toward us and the boys excitedly chased each other around the crowded store. Fala joined right in, barking and panting.

It was so precious when Sumi got a Scottish terrier just like the President's dog and used the same name. When I told her so, she had said with pride, "We have a great President. At least I can have a dog like his to remind the whole family what a wonderful country this is."

Sumi's eyes lit up when she saw me come in. "Hi, Lolly."

I gave her a little wave, saying, "I brought your Fala a bone that I saved from dinner." Opening the clasp on my purse, I unwrapped the bone from my hankie. Fala's big black nose caught the scent. He barked sharply as I said, "Here, boy." He snatched it from me and ran off to the back room away from any possible thieves.

"How's Hiroshi?" I refashioned the brim on my old spruce-green felt hat.

"He's doing well, very busy with deliveries." Sumi feather-dusted the multi-tiered shelves in the store, turning sideways so her large abdomen wouldn't get in the way. "How's your husband?"

"He works long hours at the trucking company, but I can't complain. I'm glad he has such a stable job. I hear unemployment is still very high."

"We should always count our blessings," Sumi said, always quick with a positive word.

"Mama, Mama, can I have some candy?" Edna

interrupted, pulling at my black dotted skirt, bumping my calves with the hem.

Sumi reached into one of the many round glass jars of sweets. She pulled out a bright red lollypop for Edna.

"Thanks, Mrs. Maso," she said.

"Matsumoto," I gently corrected.

Edna simply said, "Thanks."

I beamed at her and thanked Sumi again. Frankie and Billy noticed the transaction. My son demanded candy, then darted off toward the back of the store to share it with Frankie before I could reprimand him for not being grateful. The boys were the same age and matching height, but that was the only physical feature they shared. My Billy had apple-red, curly Irish hair with freckles spotting every which way all over his face. Frankie's black, shiny, shoe polish hair matched his large, crescent moon-shaped eyes, which were full of sparkles. Both the boys exuded firecracker energy.

I looked at my list and smiled at Sumi as she gathered all the items I read off. Sumi wet her finger, pushing a stray wisp of jet-black hair into her tight, well-fashioned bun roll.

"How's your brother's wife in San Pedro?" I asked, remembering she was also pregnant.

Sumi placed everything in two bags. "She's two and a half weeks late. Hiroshi and I have been praying for her."

"I will, too." I unconsciously reached into my blouse to hold my tiny gold cross. "It'll be swell for both of you to have babies almost the same age." I patted Sumi's swollen belly.

"Is your sister doing OK?" Sumi asked.

"She's still not pregnant yet after three years of trying.

I never had that problem!" I laughed as my cheeks flushed.

"That's a long time." Sumi got a broom from the corner and swept the already spotless floor.

I glanced around at the Matsumotos' store. It was cleaner than my house. It's a good thing no one ever came over to see the stormy mess in my living room.

"How did you get Frankie potty trained so early? Edna pretty much trained herself, but boys are harder to deal with, I think."

"The only trick that worked for me was to give him candy every time he went in the toilet. I'll give you some of these new candies for Billy." Sumi poured some hard-coated tiny button sweets from a cardboard tube onto the counter.

"Ooooo, they're pretty!" I admired the five different colors of candy circles.

"They're called M&M's. Here, try one." Sumi popped two into my mouth.

"Gosh, chocolate inside. Yum!"

"With so many little pieces, you can give Billy one every time he pees in the toilet, then he'll be trained like Frankie." Sumi generously handed me the tube to keep.

"Thanks! You're so clever! I've spanked him when he soils his pants, but he just keeps doing it anyway." I scratched Fala behind the ear as he licked my wedding ring. "I gotta go finish up my ironing and mending. I hope the children take long naps today."

"Thanks for the bone. Try and visit more often." Sumi wiped down the counters.

"I wish we could have a puppy, but Joe won't allow it and says the kids are enough trouble to deal with." I pushed the cart toward the door, and called Edna and Billy as Frankie and Sumi waved goodbye.

We walked the twelve long blocks toward home. I pulled on Billy's arm. "Can't you walk faster?"

Edna held tight to the two-wheeled cart. I impatiently picked Billy up and tried to push it while sticking him on my hip. He smiled, kissed my arm, satisfied that he'd gotten his way.

Edna frowned. "Hold me, too."

"Honey, drive the cart by yourself like a big girl."

Edna liked this grownup idea, but soon grew tired of it. I put Billy down and propelled it with them both hanging on. I began singing to alleviate the crankiness.

"You are my sunshine, my only sunshine. You make me happy when skies are grey. You'll never know, dear, how much I love you. Please don't take my sunshine away."

Edna chimed in, "Please don't take my sunshine away."

Feeling proud she had learned the song, I patted the top of her head and continued to sing the rest of the verses.

The jealous bug got to Billy. He squealed out, "Love you, love you, love you, dear."

After settling in back at home, I wondered if Joe might reconsider and let us get a puppy like the Matsumotos'.

Chapter 2: The Bombing

December was a wet one that year. I was looking forward to going to Mass that morning, just to get out of the house. With the children in the bath, it gave me the needed time to sew and think. I missed going to the Methodist Church with Mama and Dad. Joe's church was complicated. I never knew when to kneel or stand. I had to concentrate very hard to watch Joe, because he expected me to teach the children. The odd language, Latin, added to my confusion. The only consolation was that the red velvet kneelers felt elegant on my silk stockings. I found the Stations of the Cross, outlined in stained glass, fascinating to gaze at when I had a chance. Whenever we were at church, Billy's constant bumping and squirming annoyed me. Joe would usually give me a boyish dimpled smile, put his arm around me with a gentle squeeze, and ease my tension. When he gave me this sweet gesture it made the conversion of my faith in order to marry him worthwhile.

I rubbed Billy's sweet-smelling body dry, deep in thought as Edna tried to fashion a towel on her head. I heard Joe call to me.

"Come quick! Listen to this news."

I left the children, each wrapped up in towels, and told Edna to try and help Billy get a shirt on. Joe was in the living room turning the radio up louder.

"The first attack began at 7:33 A.M. and several more attacks have followed."

"What happened, honey?" My voice shuddered.

"The Japs have bombed Pearl Harbor. Those goddamned yellow snakes!" Joe sucked his beer from the bottle and between slugs preached to me, "We better send 'em all back to where they came from. Damn spies! They ain't true Americans like us. This is white men's country!" A beer drip ran down his chin and he wiped it off with the back of his hand.

I folded and unfolded my legs on the davenport, while Joe fiddled with the radio and tried to find a station to repeat the entire broadcast. After listening to it in its finality, I crept off into the kitchen, my hands trembling. No wonder he was drinking beer this early in the morning. I had no idea where Pearl Harbor was, but was afraid to ask. The unsightly line between my eyebrows squeezed together as I fretted. My stomach churned hard against my oatmeal breakfast. All I could think about was sweet Sumi and Frankie, the only Japanese people I knew.

"What time is it?" Joe shouted, coming into the living room.

I glanced at Dad's dark walnut clock on the mantel and thought Joe could look at it as well as I could.

"It's 9:30, dear," I murmured, wishing his fierce mood would pass.

"Get the children ready; we have to go to Mass." Joe lit up a Chesterfield, puffing away.

After church, we stayed quite a while in the parking lot. Joe hashed over the whole event with the men in his clan. I watched him clench and unclench his fists, saying

"Jap" this and "Jap" that. It made me feel uncomfortable, like he was saying a curse word in front of the church.

At home, I unpinned my worn-out hat and helped the children change into their play clothes, then went into the kitchen to start lunch. Joe sat down near the blaring radio. I heard the frightening newscast all over again as I sliced last night's roast beef much too thin.

With the children down for a nap, after Joe finished the paper, I hungrily read it.

The Federal Bureau of Investigation rounded up 737 Japanese and put them in federal custody. Couches were slit looking for evidence of enemy espionage.

"Oh, my," escaped from my mouth. I flipped the paper down. "I hope Sumi's family is OK."

"Get me a beer, Lolly. Are you talking about that Jap store you go to? Tomorrow, buy 50 pounds of sugar, and not at that slant-eye's market." He got up, dug into his pants for his wallet, took out a few dollars, then rubbed the crisp, precious bills together with his fingers as he presented them to me. "After you get the sugar, hide it under the bed and don't tell anyone." He pointed at me. "Stop shopping at that Jap store. Not one penny of my hard-earned money is going to those people!"

I held my lips together to seal in all my anger. Who would I possibly tell and why was he making me do this? It must have something to do with the bombing. Sumi was the only friend I had, and Sis was too far away now. Joe had all his buddies down at the trucking company. I turned away and bit the inside of my cheek. Blinking my eyes to push back the tears, I mumbled, "I'll check on the children."

"Get me a beer," he roared again.

There was so much I wanted to say to Joe, but I knew he wouldn't listen. It would be great if Joe's boss sent him on one of those long-distance delivery trips. I would only have to cater to the children and then I'd have time to get some interesting sewing projects done. How could Sumi and Hiroshi's store be that bad? They displayed more patriotism in their business than we did in our little home.

Watercolor by Joe Fitzgerald, age 8, 1944, Maritime Child Development Center, Richmond, CA. Courtesy Richmond Museum of History, Richmond, CA

Chapter 3: Sugar and a Loaf of Bread

After Joe left for work, I peeked outside and surmised that the creamy clouds that drifted by did not show any sign of rain. It was breezy out, and the leaves were haphazardly darting all about.

"Get your coats, let's go to Sumi's store."

"Oh, goody!" Billy threw his arms up and turned in a circle. "I can play tag with Frankie."

"I'll get more candy!" Edna clapped.

Ducking under the wind-flapping American flag at the store, I helped the children pull the door. "Sumi, I've been worried. Have the police come by?" I gripped the edge of the store counter.

"No, they didn't, but we're not afraid. We were born here and glad the police are getting rid of all the spies. Look at this article in the Japanese-American newspaper."

The Japanese empire must be defeated. The bombing of innocent women and children in a surprise attack without even a hint of declaring war can never be forgotten. These are indeed dark days; suspicion is frequently aroused because of our similarity in facial characteristics to the enemies. But, blood ties mean nothing now. We do not hesitate to repudiate and condemn our ancestral country.

There's the proof, I thought, and smiled broadly. The

Japanese-American families are just as concerned about the war as we are.

"We want to defend our country as much as you do," Sumi said, lightly pounding her fist on the counter after I gave her back the article.

"I hope other people know that." I squeezed her hand with affection. Worrisome thoughts crept upon me about Joe. "Sumi, I need sugar, and a lot of it."

"We've only 30 pounds left. Strangers have been coming in all day to buy sugar. Everyone's worried about a shortage since the bombing in Hawaii."

"Oh my, no wonder Joe wanted me to get some."

Sumi helped me put 15 pounds of sugar in the cart, gave the children each a sweet, and we started toward the door. "Thanks, Sumi. See you later."

"Bye, Lolly, take care." Sumi wiped down the counter as Frankie chased the puppy about.

Pushing the heavy cart full of sugar with both children in tow, I stopped to read a poster attached to a telephone pole down the block from Matsumotos' store.

Jap Hunting License:

Good for Duration of Hunting Season

Open Now

No Limit

"Oh my God! How can people be so cruel?" A nasty scowl formed on my face.

"What?" Edna observed my scornful expression.

"Nothing, honey. Here's a new song we can learn: 'Pardon me boys, is this the Chattanooga choo-choo...'" Singing always changed my mood. Magazine pictures of Glenn Miller flapping the mute on the mouth of his trombone flashed in my mind. The *whah, whah* noise of the train in the song waved through my mind as the wheels of the cart squeaked along. Maybe Billy would learn to play the high-spirited trombone someday.

"Woooo, wooo, Chattanooga, there you are," I belted out as we walked a few blocks to Solesky's grocery store.

"I forgot bread," I fibbed to the children as we went inside the new store.

Toward the final block home my guilt eased up after going to Solesky's. Now Joe couldn't accuse me of going to a "Jap" store.

Billy began to get cranky. I laid him on my shoulder, telling Edna, "Be a big girl, help me push the cart." I sang the same tune again so she could learn more of it.

Edna successfully joined in with her cute little voice. "Track 29, give me a shine!"

I helped her with the word "Chattanooga" as she stumbled on it. Edna sang the part, "Won't you choo-choo me home," very sweetly. The rhythmic melody soothed Billy as he sucked his thumb and fell asleep. His body fell heavy on me like a wet bag of laundry.

Before reaching home, I wondered whether I should tell the children to not mention to Joe about going to the Matsumotos' store. I never knew what he would do.

Chapter 4: How to Tell the Japs from the Chinese

A few weeks went by. I sat in the living room darning one of Edna's socks. The children slept soundly in the next room.

Joe rocked erratically in his grandfather's worn rocking chair. He waved a *Life Magazine* at me, saying, "Read this article, Lolly! 'How to tell a Jap from a Chinese.' Educate yourself in case we get invaded." Joe got up, slapped the magazine on my lap, and pointed at the pictures. He proceeded to read it to me in a condescending teacher voice. "Japanese have flattened noses, earthy yellow complexions, heavy beards, rosy pointed cheeks, eyes with less epicanthic folds.' Look here," he read, poking hard with his fat finger at the next photo of a Chinese officer. "Parchment yellow complexion, more epicanthic folds on eyes, scant beard, and never has rosy cheeks."

I looked obediently at the photographs. Japanese Army General Hideki Tojo didn't look any different than the Chinese officer. I nodded at Joe, handed him back the magazine and got busy hunting through my wicker basket of mending. He threw the magazine back on the table, reached for a cigarette, then disappeared into the bathroom. Joe was in there longer than usual, so I tuned into the "Abbott and Costello Show." He came out with a smirk on his face, right in the middle of "Who's on First?" I stared at his naked lip.

"There, see? I ain't got no more mustache like the

slant-eyes wear!" He twitched his bare lip back and forth with great satisfaction.

"I better check on the children," I said, finding an excuse not to pursue this tense subject.

Joe glanced at the clock. "It's getting late. Meet me in the bedroom."

I slunk off to the children's room, dreading going to bed. It had been a few days since we'd made love, and I was not in the mood. I rarely was. Kneeling down between the children's beds, I kissed each one above their tiny eyebrows. I bowed my head, and prayed silently to myself, Lord, protect my little ones, but please don't give me any more.

"Lolly, I'm waiting!"

I rose up on my weary feet and went into our room.

"It's about time," Joe snickered.

I pulled my housedress above my head, followed by my slip. Joe watched and gave me a low whistle. My heart quickened, delighted he still liked gazing at my saggy-after-two-children body. He pulled the covers back, signaling me in, gave me one kiss then rolled on top of me, rocking back and forth. I felt melancholy from the lecture about the Japanese, and my mind wandered elsewhere. I distracted myself from his grunting by making an extravagant grocery list in my mind: one case of Coca-Cola, a three-layer chocolate cake, ten Hershey bars, and a rack of lamb. At last he made the loudest noise as he rolled off and promptly began to snore. I couldn't sleep for the fear of getting pregnant. If only he would pull out before he came. I rose, tiptoed into the bathroom, and peed as hard as I could, flushing his seed down the toilet. There appeared to be a contest in his family as to how many children each of his siblings could bear in the least number of years. I slipped back under the blankets and tried to go to sleep.

Chapter 5: Too Much News

As soon as Joe left for work, I checked outside the door to make sure he was gone. I abandoned my chores and relaxed on the sofa to listen to the radio. I clicked my tongue and shook my head; I heard nothing but bad news for my dear friend Sumi. I made a fast breakfast of toast and juice, then got the children dressed. After I jotted down a few items on my grocery list, I made the children hurry to Sumi's by teaching them to skip down the street. Edna did well, but Billy tripped. I kissed and hugged him, and slowed down my pace.

"Hi," Sumi greeted as she reached into one of the gleaming glass jars of candy and presented a Tootsie Roll to each of the children.

"How's your family?" I frowned.

After taking my short list, she said, "Hiroshi had to go the police station and bring our box camera. We didn't have a short wave radio, but he played it safe and gave them our Zenith. When the police asked if we had any weapons or binoculars, he said 'No,' with such surprise they searched him on the spot." Sumi's eyes widened as she continued rapidly. "We don't have any guns and never needed any in this neighborhood."

"That's for sure." I nodded, then nervously cracked a knuckle.

"My brother's family in San Pedro was ordered to leave their home and fishing boat, with only two days' notice!" Sumi avoided my shocked face and glanced out the window at the majestic live oak trees.

I winced and stared at my heels, but could find no words of comfort. Frankie, Billy, and Fala chased each other around me. Grateful for the distraction, I chuckled, bent over, and petted the puppy as he slobbered on the back of my hand.

We heard the rain drumming on the roof as soon as we arrived home. Edna cuddled next to me and we looked at her favorite picture book, *Madeline*. Billy stretched out on the floor trying to build houses from an old deck of cards, but they kept falling down.

Joe came in from work. He barely said hello and snapped on the radio. I was tired of hearing bad news and tried not to listen.

"All German, Japanese, and Italians must evacuate areas on the San Francisco waterfront..."

"I'm German!" My eyes opened wide.

"You're no longer a German and don't you forget it! You've married into my clan, you're Irish now!" Joe tapped his fingers on his chair, clinking his wedding band.

To avoid any further discussion, I got up to do a tub of wash. While Joe was in the garage and with the children in bed for the night, I sat down to relax. I couldn't stop myself from picking up yesterday's newspaper. The headline read, "Executive Order 9066." Try as I might, I could not understand it. Over and over it told about the military areas, but nowhere did it mention the Japanese. I wished I could ask Joe about it. He acted smart, but his

19

slurring remarks made me feel too stupid to bother. Joe couldn't explain things to me. His answers were either too short or he went overboard yelling and shaking his finger, which caused my ears to close up. I put the newspaper down and went into the bedroom. At my dad's well-worn desk, I wrote a letter to Diana.

Dear Sis:

How are you doing during this troublesome time? The bombing of Pearl Harbor shook me up pretty bad. It's a good thing Joe made me buy a load of sugar to stash under the bed, because I hear it is now being used for gunpowder, torpedo fuel, and dynamite! Now that the U.S. has declared war, it has me in a constant state of worry.

I am friendly with a sweet Japanese gal and her three-year-old son (the same age as Billy). She owns a store that I have been shopping at for over two years now. Sumi doesn't even have a foreign accent because she was born here. She's a very patriotic person despite all the incriminating news about Japanese-Americans on the radio.

In front of her store there is an over-sized American flag on a tall pole. Why, you almost have to duck to get through the door. The Matsumotos are so American they named their son Franklin, and even got a Scottish terrier like the president's. I'm telling you, Sis, this family has Japanese eyes but an American heart.

Joe's calling me, must close. Give Edwin my regards.
Love, your Sis

Joe came in from the garage. "Lolly, it's getting late. What are you doing?"

I put the letter in an envelope, went into the kitchen in order to hide it on top of the refrigerator, then reluctantly got ready for bed.

Chapter 6: Women's Work and The Navy

Several months later, Joe bounded in from work with a surprisingly cheerful, "How's it goin'?"

Edna kissed his leg while he tousled Billy's wild red hair.

Billy felt his father's good mood. "Can you teach me jacks?"

Joe's laugh was filled with affection. "Sure, sport, you get 'em out and I'll meet you in your room."

Edna pulled at his pant leg. "Can you see how I dressed my paper dolls?"

"OK, babycakes, I'll meet you both in a minute." Joe turned all his attention on me and kissed my cheek.

Confused, I bent over to take the meatloaf out of the oven. He affectionately patted me on my bottom. I wondered why he was acting so jolly. He usually came in tired, grumpy, and desired only to be left alone. Joe hugged me from behind with his big trucker's body as I placed hot potatoes on top of the stove. I turned around and he gave me a long kiss. A warm, tingling sensation spread all over me.

Hesitantly, not wanting to break the mood, I asked, "Did you get a raise at work, honey?"

"No, I'm not going to that trucking job again!" His dimples flashed at me.

"Oh, my God. Joe, did you get fired?"

Smirking, he said, "No, stupid! I joined the Navy on my lunch hour!"

"The Navy?" My eyes suddenly grew bigger.

"I'd rather join now than wait for my number to come up." He smacked a wet one on my cheek.

I turned away from him and inspected the small cracks in the old wooden floor. "But you have a family. You can't be drafted!"

"Yesseree, the United States Navy." He tapped his fingertips together.

I chewed on a cuticle to hide the fear in my eyes.

"I'll be shipping out in a few weeks." Joe headed toward the kids' room. Laughter erupted as they all played together.

A tear escaped my eye. I dragged the dishes out and set the table. "Dinnertime," my voice quivered.

Joe came in and saw my watery eyes. "I've got to do my part to beat those Japs and Nazis." At the table, Joe bowed his head. "Lord, help this world be a safer place, in the name of the Father, the Son and the Holy Ghost."

Keeping my face low, I held in my breath, gulping to keep back the tears.

After the children were tucked into bed, we sat alone in the living room. Joe inhaled a Chesterfield and read the daily paper. I reached into my basket and began my soothing, rhythmic knitting.

That night, I embraced Joe tightly and let my tears drip down my face. Rolling the fine, curly hairs on his back with my fingers, I kissed him up and down on his neck and breathed in his maleness.

He cupped his huge hands on my face. "You know how much I love you, don't you, honey?"

"Yes, but how will I manage with Edna and Billy without you?"

"You'll be fine."

He kissed my nose, then rolled me on my back, rocking back and forth inside me. My mind drifted off, full of despair. After he finished, I turned away and tried to sleep.

Joe went to get the newspaper. Much to my surprise, he took both children with him. I couldn't remember the last time I was alone in the house. Going through the cupboard, I was eager to find all the ingredients to make a coffee cake. Joe would be pleased to have warm cake with his paper on his last day home.

When he came back, he threw down the *San Francisco Examiner* and said smugly, "Now I don't have to think about you visiting that Jap family when I'm gone."

The headline of the *Examiner* stood out in bold block letters: **OUSTER OF JAPS NEAR**

After I read the article, I was overwhelmed. I went into the kitchen and overbeat the batter. Joe came in with Billy wrapped around his leg.

"Daddy, play marbles with me."

"Let's set the table for your mother first. Get your sister."

Now Joe was doing women's work! He must be

thinking about how much he'll miss me when he leaves for the service tomorrow, I thought. After I put the cake in the oven, I watched him handing Edna the forks to put out on the table. Billy was in the corner rolling his marbles about. I sat down at the kitchen table to look over my cookbook, trying to find recipes that contained less sugar. Smelling a burning odor, I got up suddenly, opened the oven door and poked at the slightly burnt cake. Getting it out, I scraped off the black parts, and hoped Joe wouldn't notice.

In the morning, Joe wore his sparkling new uniform and kissed me passionately. The smell of the fresh new material filled me with passion. We all went to the station together. As we waited for the train, Joe kissed me. His kiss was so long and caring, I hardly felt the children smacking at our legs. Joe's boyish grin radiated excitement toward his new adventure in the Navy.

At the depot we watched the train chug away, and waved long after Joe was gone.

Billy pulled at Edna's pigtails. She screamed and pleaded with me, "Make him stop!"

I slapped Billy's hand, then grabbed it and dragged them both along toward the bus for our ride home. All I could think about was the fear of being alone with no help from Joe.

Chapter 7: The Curfew

After Joe left for the Navy, I allowed the children to sleep in my bed with me every night. His empty side of the bed felt too cold and lonely. I lay there until I couldn't stand Billy kicking me like an eggbeater.

I must train the children back to their own beds, I thought.

Joe wouldn't tolerate this arrangement. He would probably scold me, saying the children were not little babies anymore. It was much quieter now without his ranting and raving filling the house.

I slipped out to have a few moments alone, and got the morning mail. Putting the kettle on, I sat at the kitchen table and read a letter from Sis.

Dear Lolly:

I tried to understand your feelings about your Japanese friend, but the Japs are really beating the pants off of us in this war. They tricked us by planning an attack on Pearl Harbor right in the middle of peace talks. Lately, there have been severe losses of our troops in the Pacific. Someone at work said Japanese-American farmers are lighting signal fires in the fields and planting their crops in special patterns to help their fighter pilots find targets. Everyone I know says all the Japanese people are treacherous, as well as barbaric by nature. I think it is absolutely necessary to put all the Japanese-Americans in camps until this war is over. After all, we do not want an attack on our country again like Pearl

Harbor! Joe has every right to feel the way he does, but I wish he wouldn't talk to you so harshly, like I have heard him do.

Edwin was drafted a few weeks ago. We figured it would happen since we don't have children. He was going to enlist anyway. I was bored with him gone and decided to do my part and got a war job! I know how surprised you must be to read this, since I have never worked a day in my life. Now, I'm helping rivet airplanes! I rivet the fuselage (this is just a fancy word for the main body of the airplane). Oh, I forgot to tell you what riveting means. I use this heavy metal "gun" that shoots a bolt into the holes of the aircraft. I work alongside a bucker named Jesse Mankiller! She's a Cherokee Indian and uses a metal bar to bend the other end of the rivet. This whole process keeps the plane parts together. I read 12,000 American Indians left the reservations for war-related work. We joke around a lot during break time, because the noise of riveting deadens any conversation during work. It's fun and I feel like I'm doing something for the war effort. I may be doing a man's job, but I put on lipstick every day. It is required that I wear a bandana to keep my long hair back. I fashion a piece of it in the front, which gives me more of a feminine look.

President Roosevelt is requesting that 50,000 planes be built by the end of the year, so I better get busy!

I wish I could write more, but I'm falling fast asleep trying to get used to this upside down, dead man's shift (12 P.M.- 6 A.M.). Meals are so confusing!

Love, Sis

Riveter, Harriet Williams, aka Princess Hiahl-tsa, posed in her traditional dress.

I tiptoed in on the children and saw them sprawled out on my bed making sweet sleeping noises. I happily got out a few sheets of writing paper. I thought it didn't matter how long the kids napped or when they got up, because Joe was gone and time belonged solely to me.

Dear Sis:

I can't imagine you working! How do you find time to get your curls in order? You were always more of a glamour girl than me. I can't even picture you in overalls. What a stitch!

I know the Japanese are winning, but still, why should American born Japanese be punished? On the news I heard a congressman from Mississippi saying, "All Japanese should be interned whether they are so-called loyal Americans or not. I'm for catching every one of them in America and putting them in concentration camps. Let's get rid of them now!" He ended his speech adding, "Once a Jap, always a Jap." A lieutenant general then added, "It makes no difference whether a Japanese is theoretically a citizen, he is still a Japanese. Giving him a scrap of paper won't change him. I don't care what they do with the Japs so long as they keep them contained." The nastiness in the news frightens me.

I found out from Sumi what "interned" means. She said it's placing the Japanese who live here in special military camps. She is such an intelligent gal. She reads all the time. Sumi agrees with the war against Japan. Why, I read in the newspaper even the Mayor of Los Angeles believes we must continue to treat the Japanese in this country with courtesy and respect. I also read Attorney General Biddle said evacuating Japanese-Americans would be unnecessarily cruel, illegal, as well as wasteful, and there is plenty of time for the Army to decide who is a threat to our national security.

The newspaper reported Lieutenant General DeWitt

saying, "An American citizen is, after all, an American citizen. I think we can weed the disloyal out of the loyal and lock them up if necessary."

The FBI, office of Naval Intelligence, and the Federal Communication Commission all informed Roosevelt that Japanese-Americans pose no security threat, but he signed Executive Order 9066 anyway, which will enforce internment. I've been staying informed by reading the newspaper and listening to the radio as often as I can. I am so worried for my friend Sumi.

Joe hates all Japanese and would curse about them all the time. Before he enlisted, I had to lie to him about going to "that Jap" store to visit my friend.

Well, Diana, enough politics for now, I love you dearly, but I don't agree with you or Joe and have a need to inform you about the other side of this issue.

By the way, have you had any morning sickness? This is the first sign of pregnancy. Maybe you should feel lucky not having the responsibility of children to raise alone like I do during these troubled times. Have you heard from Edwin? In a way, I miss the rousing arguments we used to have because it was stimulating and we do have a deep respect for each other's opinions in the long run.

Miss you,
Love Always, Lolly

When I opened the front door, I saw the cloudless blue sky announcing spring was just around the corner. With renewed energy I said to the kids, "Wake up, sleepyheads. Let's visit Sumi and Frankie."

I had felt too weak to visit her before. The possibility of internment was in the news constantly, making me fear Sumi's situation was becoming hopeless.

Edna clapped her small hands together. "I'll get the cart by myself."

I reached for our coats. "We don't need any groceries this time." As much as I missed Joe, it was such a comfort to be able to visit Sumi, even when we didn't need any food.

On the way there, I read a large, menacing sign:

Japs don't let the sun shine on you here:
KEEP MOVING!

I held my horror within in order to not disturb the children. Upon reaching the Matsumotos' store, I saw a white banner with bold, handmade capital letters stretched across the window high above the door that screamed:

WE ARE AMERICAN!

I blinked several times as I read the emblazoned sign, knowing the impending possibility of Sumi's family's internment. Ducking under the flag, Billy and Edna ran free from my shaking hands into the store without me.

Billy dashed in and yelled, "Frankie, Frankie, I have marbles!"

Sumi smiled at me. "Hi, glad you came. I needed someone to talk to."

"What's new?" I tried to act calm and adjusted my hat.

"We have a curfew now." Sumi avoided my eyes as

she rearranged the shelves.

"A curfew?"

"All Japanese have to stay inside between nine at night and six in the morning and are not allowed to travel more than five miles from home. Now Hiroshi can't make his deliveries and we have to be extra careful with money." Sumi focused on polishing the glass candy jars with a cloth.

I combed my fingers around Fala's thick, muscular neck as he panted around my skirt.

"Would you like some tea?" Sumi rapidly changed the subject.

"I'd love some." My mind filled with worry, wishing I could do something for her.

Sumi placed a tan, burled mahogany tray in the middle of the store. The pedestal base curved elegantly on the floor. I helped her move the chairs since she carried so much extra weight due to her pregnancy. She put a lovely Japanese patterned teapot next to the inlaid lotus leaf in the middle of the table.

"What a marvelous piece of furniture this is." I was desperately trying to cheer up the situation.

"Thanks, it's been in my family a long time. My mother brought it over on the boat; it only has one chip underneath." Sumi felt under the tray. She poured the tea into two delicate cups.

There must not be much business if Sumi is serving tea smack in the middle of the store, I thought. I searched the shelves, trying to remember if I needed any groceries, but since Joe left I'd stopped cooking big meals. The children certainly didn't care.

"How's your husband?" Sumi asked.

"I've only gotten one letter from him, and he didn't really say."

"I'll pray for his safety." Sumi adjusted her beige tent dress over her knees and sipped her tea.

"Thanks," I said, thinking her family needed more prayers than mine.

Edna came over to us, bored with watching the boys throw playing cards. "Can I've some candy?"

I spoke fast before Sumi could answer. "No, Edna. It'll ruin your appetite for lunch."

Edna kept whining, "Please, please."

Before I could protest, Sumi said, "Just one piece won't hurt."

Edna spoke in her adorable voice quite clearly. "Thanks, Mrs. Matsumoto."

I proudly cuddled her on my lap. Sumi and I chatted about the weather, my sister, and anything that had no worry attached to it. After we finished our tea, I said, "I do need a few items."

"But…you didn't bring your cart."

"I forgot it." My eyes wandered out toward the walnut trees. A single robin moved about in the branches.

As I tucked a grocery bag full of odds and ends under my arm, I knew buying these few items wouldn't really help Sumi's family.

On the way home I saw a new sign:

1 flat iron= 2 steel helmets

1 set of golf clubs= .30 caliber machine gun

70 toothpaste tubes= radiator for an army truck

DO YOUR PART!

A few days later there was another letter from Diana, but still not a word from Joe. I read it while the children listened to the radio.

Dear Lolly:

I love my job and having my own money to spend as I wish. Too bad there is so much being rationed right now. I can't even buy a nice pair of silk stockings and hate wearing these cotton ankle socks. Whenever I get a day off, I go to the movie theater. I just saw Casablanca. *It had all the ingredients of the swellest movie: intrigue, mystery, danger, and romance! That Humphrey Bogart sure is dreamy. I got goose bumps when he said, "Here's lookin' at you, ...kid!"*

Lately, we have been riveting the B-17 Flying Fortress. This is a huge airplane that can carry ten-man crews as well as bomb loads. I was told it is equipped with gunner turrets so the crew can fight and fly at the same time. Edwin is training to be a pilot in the Army Air Corps. When I rivet, I think of him and do a very careful job, because I wouldn't want my husband piloting an airplane that wasn't properly put together.

President Roosevelt is requesting 50,000 warplanes be built, so this factory is churning 'em out 24 hours a day! You should see me in my pinstriped canvas apron and rose-flowered turban. You would bust a gut laughing!

I have enclosed a newspaper article about your famous sister. We were hootin' and hollerin' the whole time as we frantically riveted.

Lolly, using a rivet gun is just like sewing. Remember when we would take turns sewing twin dresses with Mother's machine? I wish I still had my dress, just to look at the fabric from back then. Do you have the photograph Dad took of us in our dresses with his Brownie camera?

This airplane plant is as big as a small town, and the noise of constant production can be quite nerve-racking. When I get home the sound of riveting continues to ring in my ears. I do love all the camaraderie at work and have oodles of new friends.

Must dress now and hurry off to work,
Write soon,
Love, Diana
P.S. Kiss the kids for me.

I unfolded the cutout newspaper article enclosed with the letter.

Two Women Drive New Rivet Record

Diana Turner and her bucker Adeline Ellison drove a record 3,345 rivets into the wing of a Grumman Avenger Torpedo Bomber while working the midnight-to-six shift. This is a new record for the history of riveting. Mrs. Edwin Turner reports, "Running a rivet gun is no different than running a sewing machine. It does build up the arms more, though!"

Folding the letter, I tried to picture my sophisticated, high-fashioned sister, who usually wore the latest hat, in a turban and apron with a rivet gun. The thought caused me

35

to burst out laughing.

I felt that my sister sure was lucky to have such an interesting job and lots of friends to interact with all the time. Although I felt a sense of freedom with Joe gone, I missed his discipline, which kept the children in order. I had trouble keeping a routine and the house was a mess. It was a little too quiet without him. I worried that if Sumi left, I'd have no one to talk to.

Riveting

Chapter 8: Only One Suitcase

The next morning, the children played peacefully as I listened to the radio and sorted through my sewing. I found a few yards of navy striped percale and matching rickrack trim. I had bought the material by saving up spare change from the money Joe used to give me each week for groceries. Now that he was gone I had a little bit more leisure time, but less money. It wasn't that long ago that I had wished Joe had a long-distance trucking job to keep him away for a while. Now, I was beginning to feel lonely.

The radio bellowed out:

"All Japanese branch banks are now closed.

The US treasury has frozen all their bank accounts, only $100.00 a month can be withdrawn.

All people of Japanese ancestry must secure or sell their houses."

This alarming broadcast made me change my plans. I put away the material and I called the children toward the door.

The cool spring air turned Billy's chubby cheeks to a rosy red. The month of May was slightly overcast with the usual coastal fog. We passed by the lone cherry blossom tree on the block.

Billy pointed to it. "Pink popcorn!"

I held his hand delightfully. "It's a cherry tree."

His face full of wonder, he asked, "It'll make cherries?"

Edna answered cutely, "Yummy, yummy, cherries!"

At Johnny's Five and Dime, I saw a startling sign displayed across the window that screamed:

NO JAPS WANTED HERE!

The Jenkins furniture store had a cardboard sign on its door:

JAPS, KEEP MOVING. THIS IS WHITE MAN'S NEIGHBORHOOD!

Rounding the corner, at the Matsumotos' store below the "WE ARE AMERICAN" sign hung a new one just as large:

CLOSING OUT, EVACUATION SALE

Billy and Edna pulled the door before I could compose myself.

Upon hearing the brass bell ring, Sumi waddled out as I shouted, "What's going on, Sumi?" even though I suspected the Matsumotos' end must be near. My eyes shot about the empty shelves as I wondered how all the items could have been sold so fast, until I saw the absurdly low prices attached to the few cans left.

Sumi's bottom lip trembled. "We've just ten days to pack up and leave."

I reached and held her unsteady hand. "I'll help you pack."

"I, I don't need any help." She fidgeted with the items on the bare shelf. "Come upstairs and have some tea while I sort. We have 15 years of stuff to go through and we're only allowed one suitcase each to bring."

I heard her sniffle while we climbed the narrow staircase. The children noisily chatted behind, overjoyed to explore new territory.

The living room had piles and piles of clothes, books, and mementos all scattered about. There were balls of yarn, boxes of tattered letters, family photos, Christmas and birthday cards. There was not one piece of furniture in the entire room.

"Sorry, there's nowhere to sit," Sumi said with a whisper.

The walls still had beautiful Japanese paintings tastefully displayed upon the print wallpaper.

"These paintings are magnificent!" I felt the unique textured paper of the ones that were not framed.

After watching me, Sumi said, smiling shyly, "It's rice paper."

"I've never seen any drawings like these, so detailed." I examined one depicting a scene in Japan. The trees swayed magically with the clouds; a teahouse with multiple archways reached to the sky. The figures going toward it were similar to Sumi and her husband. Even though the painting was in black, it didn't need color to express itself.

"Thanks. I painted that one when Hiroshi and I visited his parents in Japan a few years ago."

"You're incredibly talented." I explored all the paintings that hung on the living room wall.

As my eyes darted at the mounds of the Matsumotos' possessions, Sumi's words of "only one suitcase each" echoed in my mind.

"My God, Sumi, you're only allowed one suitcase each? How can you pack your entire life in one bag?"

"Like my husband says, we may have to leave most of our possessions behind, but we still have our dignity and memories to bring with us. *Shikate ga nai.'*"

"What?" I had never heard Sumi speak Japanese before. It sounded blasphemous. I nervously peered around, suspicious an FBI agent might jump right out from the closet.

"It cannot be helped," she translated, holding back her tears stoically. "Hiroshi had to call the junk man, who gave us a pittance for all our furniture. I filled out our income tax form, but didn't have money to pay the taxes. Now I can pay the balance after selling everything."

"Where are… are they… sending you?" I stammered.

"San Bruno."

"Will you write?" I asked, my voice catching as I tried to hold back my emotions.

"If we're allowed."

My teacup rattled as my hand shook. I was too astonished, and couldn't find any comforting words to say. Fala went to each pile, sniffed, and enjoyed all the new smells on the floor. He rolled a beautiful little doll with his large black button nose toward my foot.

Sumi shouted, "Don't, Fala!"

He obediently moved away.

I picked up the remarkably detailed four-inch figure, feeling the smooth ceramic head. The body felt a bit squishy. "What a precious doll." I smoothed down the doll's green embroidered dress.

"Thanks. This collection was handed down from my mother for *Hinamatsuri*." When she saw my questioning face she added, "Japanese Girl's Day. Every year on March 3rd we display these Hina dolls. Here, I'll show you."

Sumi arranged the many dolls on a five-tiered platform that was covered with red felt. Gushing with pride, she explained all the colorful figures to Edna and me. She sat with her legs folded beneath her in a dignified Japanese fashion. "Here's the Emperor and Empress on the top tier, next come all the attendants in their court dress."

The Emperor, the tallest doll, was about a foot in height and wore a purple silk costume. The Empress was shorter and adorned in stunning red silk with tassels. All the other characters were about half that size.

On the third tier, Sumi arranged five male musicians with hand-painted, whimsical expressions and exquisitely detailed instruments. Next she placed near the musicians a beautiful female singer wearing a hair ornament and holding a one-inch, finely crafted Japanese fan. There remained quite a pile of accessories on the floor; a lovely cherry tree, a tiny sewing kit, and even dishes for a tea ceremony.

I picked up a figure that sported a fierce, animated

pose. The warrior doll held a miniature bow and arrow. "What's inside the body?"

"They're packed with rice straw. I used to love playing with all the extra decorations." Sumi fingered one of the tiny teacups. "If I have a baby girl, I'll pass the collection on to her." Sumi moved her hand over her round belly, adjusting her dress. "The dolls possess the power to contain bad spirits. Long ago, they used to be set afloat on a boat down a river to the sea to take the evil spirits with them. Now, *Hinamatsuri* is a time to pray for a young girl's growth and happiness."

"They're so charming."

"Some girls had as many as seven platforms with even more accessories than I have."

Edna helped Sumi with the arrangement.

"Could you store my collection until I get back?" Sumi's dark eyes pleaded.

"I think so." I hesitated, wondering where could I safely hide them from Joe when he came back on leave.

Edna held one of the Hina dolls. "I could play with them every day!"

Seeing Sumi's concerned expression, I said, "No, Edna."

Sumi interrupted, "You could help your mom in March, set them up for *Hinamatsuri*, and then they must be safely put away."

Edna clasped another doll with excitement, not knowing the month of March had just recently passed. Besides, Sumi might be back by then. Sumi wrapped all the dolls and accessories with care in old Japanese newspaper.

Edna and I helped.

"I need another favor of you." She placed the last figurine in the box.

"Anything, Sumi," I said, trying to relieve the heavy burden of guilt resting within me of her impending internment by my race.

"It's Fala." A small tear escaped from her beautifully shaped eyes. She wiped it away and forced a smile on her face.

"Umm," I answered as I thought about Joe once again.

"You know we can't take him with us."

Edna caught on to the conversation. "Mommy, we need a dog!"

I looked at Sumi's sorrowful face and reluctantly agreed. "We could use a watch dog with Joe gone, but it would only be temporary." I stroked Edna's soft, sandy colored hair.

"What is temporary?" Edna asked, hugging Fala so tightly that he yelped.

"Fala belongs to the Matsumotos. They're going away for a little while and only need us to take care of him until they come back."

"Like a vacation?" she asked and released the squirming puppy.

"Kind of," I said.

3/13/42

Photograph by Dorothea Lange, Oakland, California

Chapter 9: A Victory Visitor

As the months went by, I had gotten used to living without my husband. It was naptime, my favorite two hours of the day that belonged only to me. I went through my sewing basket. When the pincushion fell out, Fala picked it up, being the alert and fast-moving dog that he was.

"Drop it, Fala!" He obeyed as I scratched behind his pointed ear. He barked, which made me realize I had forgotten to feed him that morning. I went into the bedroom, crouched down, and retrieved one of the many cans of dog food that I had hidden under the bed.

A tear dribbled down my cheek as I twisted the can opener. I placed the lid in the garbage. Fala caught a whiff of the food and ran around me until I scraped it into a bowl. He gobbled it up. I blew my nose and felt heavy-hearted. I missed Sumi, my only friend, who had been taken away. Fala licked my hand, as though trying to comfort me with his doggy smile. Finally, he settled down at my feet. I sat staring around the much too quiet house. A few minutes went by as I lectured myself to stop feeling sad, and prayed for a letter from Sumi.

I checked in on the children and watched Billy making soothing sucking noises with his thumb in his mouth. Edna's eyes fluttered, lost in dreamland. I placed a smart floral material on the kitchen table and searched through my pattern box. There were two patterns, one for me and one for Edna. The two dresses were similar. I could rework them to make twin mother and daughter dresses.

I turned up the radio and pinned the patterns on the material. There was a national debate about the possibility of forcing women to work, a possible draft. One of the men said quite fervently, "The more women at work, the sooner we will win."

With my long, heavy shears I cut through the material. The smell of the fresh fabric excited me as I looked forward to my new sewing adventure. I hummed along with a sweet new ditty on the radio. The "Oklahoma" song sure was catchy.

The dog began barking furiously.

"Fala, stop barking!"

I heard a knock on the front door. Patting Fala on the head, I said, "Good boy!"

I glanced around, picked up a stray sock, and put all the dishes in the sink. Who could it be? I opened the door just a crack and looked out. A lovely lady in a smart, man-tailored tan and white striped suit with a badge on her lapel that read "Victory Visitor" stood smiling at me with her shiny red lips.

"Good afternoon, I'm a Victory Visitor, my name is Mrs. Stephens." She adjusted her well-pressed jacket.

"Hi, Mrs. O'Brien, please come in." I unconsciously adjusted my ordinary housedress.

"I'd love to. What a charming house you have, and it's in such a nice neighborhood," she gushed with politeness.

"Thanks. Care for a cup of coffee?" I glanced over at my sewing mess spread out all over the table.

"I'd love a cup. What a lovely print that material

has!" She slid her hand over the fabric. "I'm happy to see that you sew."

"I enjoy it. I read about Victory Visitors in last month's issue of *Ladies Home Companion*. I'd like to work for the war effort, but I have two small children and my husband's in the Navy." I filled the percolator with water and turned up the stove flame.

"I saw your blue star in the window. My husband's in the Navy, too," Mrs. Stephens said.

"Where's he stationed?"

"Somewhere in the Pacific." She frowned.

"So is mine. Too bad we never know exactly where." I bit one of my cuticles off, folded up my pattern and placed the material in the basket. "Have a seat. I'll get the coffee. Would you care for cream and sugar?"

"Cream please, I'd better skip the sugar. I've been trying to do without it since the scarcity. You know, Mrs. O'Brien, with most of our men away, our country is having a great deal of trouble trying to produce all that is needed to win this war." She overflowed with enthusiasm.

"I've heard about the labor shortage, but my mom always told me that the first duty of a mother is to be with her children." I wished I had on my two-toned shirtwaist dress instead of my plain housedress. Unfastening the top button and re-buttoned it again I said, "My kids are only three and four, I can't go to work."

"There's a retired schoolteacher right nearby who will take in neighborhood children so housewives can work."

"Nearby?" I questioned, my eyes widening.

"Mrs. Crabtree does a great job with the little ones,

and with your fine sewing ability you'd make a wonderful welder."

"I don't even know what welding is." I gulped my hot coffee.

"Welding is just like sewing pieces of fabric together, but instead of thread, you put a strip of bead to join two pieces of sheet metal." Mrs. Stephens continued with a matter-of-fact air, "Women can become soldiers just like our men, but production soldiers. Besides, it would only be for the duration of the war, then we can all go back to being housewives."

I got up to pour another cup of coffee, avoiding eye contact.

Mrs. Stephens persisted. "There are evening classes in welding at Richmond High School. You can practice, get a certificate and a job at the shipyards."

"At night?" A worry wrinkle formed between my eyebrows.

"The training program is only a month and Mrs. Crabtree does watch children at night. She even gives them dinner and a bath. After class all you'd have to do is just transfer them back to their own beds. Just think, you can make $1.20 an hour when you pass!" Her voice raised an octave higher.

"That much?" I was barely scraping by with the pittance Joe sent me, and I never knew when it would come.

Chapter 10: Welding/A New Beginning

I was excited to get admitted into the welding class at Richmond High, but I had trouble concentrating. My mind would drift off, worrying about how the children were doing at Mrs. Crabtree's and what Joe would say about my taking the class.

"It's quite simple to build a ship. You get your plan, cut out your pattern, and then prefabricate it." Mr. Cunningham said this with a broad smile on his face in front of a class filled mostly with girls. "Women have a natural expertise using their hands," he said as his eyes gazed toward me.

I tried to focus on the lecture and felt uncomfortable thinking about another man besides my Joe. The teacher's smooth-toned voice was very attractive.

"A skilled welder can make a good solid seam almost anywhere—horizontal, vertical, overhead, and on angles. Welding is the basic glue of steel shipbuilding. Now, class, here are some sound slides on how to weld."

Mr. Cunningham turned on the projector, flipped off the lights, and chuckled, "Sorry, no popcorn."

I was glad when the lights went off and the slides came on because I couldn't stop staring at the instructor. He was quite a looker, even though he wore glasses. I adored having the opportunity to openly watch a man and get away with it. Not only was he handsome, but he was funny too!

His thick glasses probably gave him the Army deferred status of 4F, but his black, well-trimmed, wavy hair and quick mustached smile made up for them.

My old high school had been converted almost overnight into a well-equipped welding school. We practiced our new skill daily with leftover scrap metal.

During one class, Mr. Cunningham made an announcement: "There is now a new school available for those of you ladies needing care for your young children. Thanks to our own Henry J. Kaiser, the founder of the shipyards, he has helped subsidize the United States Maritime Commission to build the Maritime Child Development Center."

I raised my hand enthusiastically. "Where is it located?"

Mr. Cunningham beamed at me. "Let's see, I have a few pamphlets here." He glanced at one. "It's on Florida Ave. and Harbour Way right near the shipyards. I'll pass these out for anyone who needs one."

I did feel guilty leaving the children with the lady down the street. But enrolling Edna and Billy in a real school, now that would be a wonderful solution for all of us. How could I sit home and sew dresses, becoming gray with worry about the war? After all, it was only temporary. Like I heard the other gals in class saying, "It's only for the duration."

On the last night of class, Mr. Cunningham gave out certificates to those who had passed. I was sweating it the whole time, until I heard, "Lauretta O'Brien." As he called my name and shook my hand, relief, as well as pride, flushed all over my body.

"Hattie Calhoun, congratulations."

The large colored gal next to me scrambled from her seat, giving Mr. Cunningham a huge grin as her eyes twinkled. She appeared so overjoyed that I reached over and shook her hand after she sat down.

With a southern drawl she said, "Why, thank ya, ma'am."

I grinned, thinking I had never been called "ma'am" before.

On the night city bus, I felt toasty in my leather work slacks. It was the first pair of pants I had ever owned. All I had to do now was pass the ship-adaptability test; then I could get my first job. From the window in the bus, I could see more activity in Richmond than I had ever seen before. There were so many different looking people moving about now. I thought about the friendly Negro girl in my class and smiled.

When I picked up the children, I told Mrs. Crabtree I would be enrolling them in the new school that Mr. Cunningham had told us about in class. I made a mental note to read the pamphlet when I got home.

The next morning, I awoke early to prepare for my new adventure. Going through my welding notebook, I found the school pamphlet. I was happy it was so close to the shipyards. I felt anxious after reading that all children accepted must be potty-trained.

"Hurry! Today's your first day at the child development center," I said to the kids as I frantically ironed Billy's pants.

Edna twirled the end of her straight hair, looked up at me with her adorable blue eyes, and asked, "What's that?"

"It's a school for children." I put the iron on the stove, then pulled off Billy's stinky night diaper and pinned on a fresh one. "Edna, don't mention anything about Billy's diapers when we get there. I can't have them turning us away; I have to work. Why are you still in your nightgown? We've a bus to catch!"

"OK, I'll get dressed real fast, then help Billy."

I touched her right dimple and smiled. "You're such a good helper. I'm glad you were born before Billy."

Getting on my new boy's-sized work shoes, I watched Edna help Billy get dressed. "Thank you, sweetie."

"Arthur's bringing a new toy to Mrs. Crabtree's!" Billy said.

"I told you we're not going there again. You're going to a new place, a school."

He began sucking his thumb, not understanding a word I had said.

"And don't suck your thumb. People don't like to see big boys doing that."

Billy dragged along, whining about not seeing Arthur; however, when I mentioned we had to take a bus, his bright blue eyes shone and he walked along the city blocks much faster.

Cuddling with him on the bus seat, I worried about the kids going to the new school. It was closer to the

53

shipyard and I was glad. In case of an emergency, like the children getting sick, they could reach me faster than at Mrs. Crabtree's. Also, it would be a nicer place for Edna to make more friends her age. At the same time, I knew it would be a huge place and I worried that the kids might get neglected there.

Chapter 11: The Child Development Center

Through the bus window, I anxiously stared at the freshly painted school building. It was quite large. The nautical windows added a whimsical touch and a friendliness to the structure.

Edna pointed excitedly exclaiming, "Look, Mom, swings."

When we got off the bus, the children released my hands and ran to the door. After I pulled it open, Billy's eyes got wider and he sucked his thumb while hiding behind my leg. Edna held on to my hand as I slowly approached the long, wooden front counter.

"Good morning. Welcome to the Maritime Child Development Center," an overly cheerful young receptionist greeted us.

Edna squished my hand so hard I pulled it away from her. She grabbed my pant leg instead. Billy jumped up and down yelling, "Up, Mama, up," hitting my other leg, turning my face redder by the minute.

A prim older lady wearing a proper, small-print frock came toward us.

"I'm Mrs. Ginzberg, the director."

As soon as I said, "Mrs. O'Brien," she bent all the way down to the children's faces, ignoring me. She spoke to them in a low voice.

"What a pretty dress you're wearing. What's your

name?"

Edna mumbled, "Edna," and picked her nose.

"I'm Billy!"

"Tell me, Billy, what is your favorite toy?"

"I have marbles and jacks."

Mrs. Ginzberg smiled widely. "Do you have any pets?"

"We have Fala," Edna added brightly. "It's a borrowed dog."

I covered up that subject by asking, "Do the children have to have shots before coming here?"

Mrs. Ginzberg rose from her bent knees and proudly announced, "We have a pediatrician on staff, he'll take care of the immunizations."

I glanced curiously at the round, yellow porthole-like windows, the child-size drinking fountains, and small chairs.

Mrs. Ginzberg proceeded to show us around the large school. There were children's paintings covering every inch of the walls, as well as most of the windows. Billy went up to an easel, looked into a milk bottle full of paint, grabbed a paintbrush, and spattered paint all over a sheet of paper.

I managed to get it from him, slapped his hand, and scolded, "Billy, don't touch other people's things!"

Mrs. Ginzberg, startled by my slapping, reprimanded me. "Mrs. O'Brien, we do not allow hitting here."

I sheepishly looked at the gleaming new wooden floor.

The director announced, "Come, children, let's go to

the library corner. Mrs. O'Brien, please fill out these registration forms. You can use the pen on the front counter."

Billy and Edna took her hands and went into another classroom.

My mind wandered as I filled out the papers. I had to keep my children disciplined and they naturally needed a swat as a reminder once in a while. Joe certainly agreed with me on that. Children had to be controlled or they became like little animals, roaming free all over the place. Mrs. Ginzberg's idea of not slapping unruly children was ridiculous. It made me wonder about that place. I had seen Mrs. Crabtree spank a naughty child when I picked up the kids the previous week.

I'd like to know how this gigantic day care is going to keep order, I thought. All I know is children must be kept in line to grow up to be productive adult citizens. That's what Dad used to say.

I left the forms at the front desk and went into the classroom. I noticed shelf after shelf of children's books. On a large hooked rug sat a circle of children. The teacher was reading with an animated voice. She paused and showed all the kids the pictures. Edna and Billy were quietly enthralled as they listened to her.

Back at the front office, I handed Mrs. Ginzberg the packet I had filled out saying, "I hope my kids do all right here."

"I'm certain they will. This is one of the newest centers, just built. All our teachers come from UC Berkeley, which offers the best education. Your children will learn many subjects here, including manners and social skills. Tomorrow, come a half hour early so the children can have their examination and shots at the pediatrician's office." She filed the papers in the cabinet.

"I'd better go, I have a test to take," I said, and glanced at a nautical, anchor-shaped clock. I looked longingly back toward Billy and Edna's classroom. There were rows and rows of brand new toys. Maybe all the children there were well behaved because there was so much to do.

After Mrs. Ginzberg left, I handed the receptionist a bag for Billy and told her it was clothes, even though it just contained diapers.

Saying goodbye at the child care center

Chapter 12: The Shipyard-adaptability Test

At the hiring hall, there must have been over 1,200 people buzzing about. All the different colors and languages of the people there startled my eyes as I tried to take it all in.

Searching about, I found a sign:

Shipyard-adaptability Test Station #1

I stood in a long line. After a half-hour went by, finally I was first in line. A cigar-smoking man with an "I dare you look" said, "Here lady, take this 25-pound bucket of scrap metal and carry it all around the room."

Beads of sweat sprouted on my nose as I circled the room, then made it back and tried to hand it to the large barrel-chested man. He narrowed his eyes, bit hard on his cigar, pointed to the floor, put a check mark on my test card and handed it back to me yelling, "Next!"

"Where do I go now?" I whispered, out of breath.

He thrust his thumb toward the right, barking at the next gal.

I got in another line and watched the gal in front of me clamber up and down a seemingly endless ladder that was against the wall. When it was my turn, a man with a stopwatch monitored my time. Afterward, I huffed, puffed and reached out for my card as the boss leered at my heaving breasts.

I grabbed my card and rushed away, deciding not to ask him where the next station was.

The card showed I had passed the adaptability test and now I had to face more lines to get my badge. While standing there, I heard two old men speaking loudly. One said, "Women are a lazy and shiftless bunch, they don't know how to work, and make all the men around them just as useless."

His creepy-faced friend agreed. "Every skirt in the yard should be given her quit slip. They neither have the brains nor the strength of us men!"

I backed away from them as far as possible. When my turn came, I showed my birth certificate and received my social security number. The photographer took my picture so fast I never got a chance to smile. The celluloid badge had a lot of information on it, including my fingerprints. I stopped at the last station, War Bonds. This boy was a sweetheart as he explained to me with great patience how much I would earn on the job. He asked me questions about dependents and how much money I received from Joe, and then suggested what amount I should spend on bonds.

Watercolor by Donald, age 10, 1944, "Outfitting Dock, Richmond Kaiser Shipyard." Courtesy Richmond Museum of History, CA

Exhausted but satisfied, I walked the long blocks to the Maritime Child Development Center to pick up the children. I watched Edna sweeping imaginary dirt with a child-size broom into a dustpan held by another little girl. There were so many children, yet no fighting like I had seen at Mrs. Crabtree's.

Edna saw me. "I made lots of friends. Can we come back?" she asked.

"We sure will." I hugged her sweet little body as her pigtails swung about. "Let's get your brother."

Edna waved at her friend. "See you tomorrow," she called out.

In Billy's classroom we watched him ramming a truck through small, wooden, multi-shaped blocks. He growled at us. "Go away."

Glancing around me, I lowered my voice. "Don't talk to me that way or you're gonna get it. Where's your coat? We've a bus to catch."

Billy drove his dump truck farther away from us. "I'm sleeping here, like Peter."

Before I could discipline him, Mrs. Ginzberg came into the room. "Hello, Mrs. O'Brien, how was your day?"

"Fine, thanks." I tried to cool my hot temper.

"I'd like a word with you before you leave."

"Has Billy been bad?" I hastily asked.

"No, he's behaving as well as three-year-olds do. His toileting is what I need to discuss with you."

I pinched my lips together, my eyes downcast.

"Mrs. O'Brien, Billy is a smart boy, but we both need

63

to get him toilet trained."

My face turned redder by the minute as she continued.

"I want you to go to the store, buy at least two playsuits with drop seats and big buttons. That way Billy can undo them himself. Those tiny, concealed buttons are too difficult for his fingers to unfasten." She tapped a finger on her hip as she spoke to me.

I glanced at the clock. "We must go catch the bus." I tried snatching Billy's hand to move him from the classroom, but he ran away from me.

Mrs. Ginzberg went up to him, knelt down, and said, "Billy, would you like to borrow a small truck, just for the night, to play with at home?"

His eyes brightened as she placed the toy into his hands. I led him easily toward the door, and said, "Thanks, Mrs. Ginzberg."

"You're welcome. Remember, roomy buttonholes. Don't forget to get your dinner to bring home. It's meat loaf and baked potatoes today." She marched off to her office.

"Thanks, Mrs. Ginzberg."

As we stood on the long dinner line, I was grateful that I didn't have to go home and cook, but the children were very unruly. I certainly had no time to get new pants for Billy. Mrs. Ginzberg had no concept of what it was like to be a working mother. I hoped I could avoid her tomorrow so she wouldn't know that I hadn't bought the pants.

Chapter 13: A Horse Stable

At the center the next morning, I dropped off the children quickly and successfully avoided Mrs. Ginzberg.

After walking to the shipyard, I stood in the long line to get into work, with my badge proudly displayed on the front of my work jacket. I felt quite pleased with myself that I had passed all the tests. The jacket was the smallest men's size I could find, which hung all over me. It was darn hot to wear all that leather in the summer and it would only get hotter when I started welding. Gazing about the line, there were mostly girls. The boys must have been 4F status. Some walked with limps, others wore glasses. They they appeared to be quite an ugly crew.

There were four large Kaiser Richmond shipyards; I was assigned to yard one. I wound my way through the crowds of workers and got to the *SS Red Oak Victory Ship*. I followed a group of people up a temporary, narrow ladder. On the first deck, I watched with fascination the beginnings of the ship being built below me. The huge metal keel was swarming with hardhats, like ants on a candy wrapper. Above me I was encompassed by seven stories of an intricate crisscross pattern of wooden framework. The hull was being constructed and was held in place by support stocks.

A mean-looking foreman sized me up and snarled, "Where's yer hardhat, lady? No standin' around without a hardhat. Follow me."

I grasped my welder's helmet tightly as we passed

through all the workers and equipment.

Then he said, "This is where you'll start."

SEPTEMBER 13, 1942 — A.M.

Building the hull at Marinship, CA, September, 1942

After the foreman left, I put on the helmet he had given me and lamely stood watching the person in front of me weld. I wondered if this was a male or female? I couldn't tell by the big welder's outfit. Besides, he or she was crouched down. The welder stepped back, pushed up the hood to examine the work, and knocked into me.

"S'cuse me, ma'am," a young girl with a velvet chocolate face exclaimed.

"That's OK, sorry I got in your way. Hey, aren't you the gal who was in my welding class?" I shouted over the hammering sounds on the steel and the hiss of the welding equipment.

"Why, sure 'nough! Name's Hattie." She smiled and exposed a mouthful of teeth.

"Lolly's mine, I'm glad I'll be working with another girl instead of some bossy boy who'd make me feel nervous."

"I know whacha y'all mean!" She put her hood down to finish her beading strip.

Time flew by when we worked together as a team. I thoroughly enjoyed performing my newfound skill as a welder.

The noon whistle blew and we headed toward a makeshift break room. Hattie went to her locker and got out her lunch bag. I went to mine, put in my gloves and hood, and shyly said, "I've got to find the canteen. I forgot my lunch."

As I found my way across the bustling shipyard, whirley cranes moved over my head, and people traveled around every which way as truck horns blared. I walked by a group of boys.

One whistled and hooted, "Hey, babe whatcha doin' tonight?"

Another added, "Hey, sugar, are you rationed?"

I turned bright red and wondered what in heaven's

name could make me that alluring in my welder's duds. I tried the ignoring technique, hoping they would stop their taunting, then beat it to the canteen line. I got the huge "riveters special" for 40 cents, which consisted of two sandwiches, salad, an apple, a pastry, and a cup of hot soup. An oriental man waited on me. There was a homemade label pinned on his jacket which read: I AM CHINESE. He handed me my lunch, and a Chinese lady took my money.

After seeing the canteen workers, I remembered I had a letter from Sumi in my pants pocket. I had been too tired to read it last night after standing in lines at the store trying to find a scarce box of laundry soap, then picking up the children from the center. Welding was enjoyable, but shopping afterwards was such a chore. Buying staples with ration coupons was no easy task. Even when I did have the coupon, I never knew what would be left to buy, anyway.

I unfolded Sumi's letter and sipped the comforting soup.

To my dear friend Lolly:

I'm sorry I haven't written sooner. I had to find the strength of a "good mood" in order to send you this letter.

The bus brought us to the Tanforan racetrack just outside the city. The cramped quarters of the stable barely hold the three of us. The first few days here I threw up constantly from the reeking stench of horse manure that rose from the floor. It seeps out of the ground between the one-inch spaces of the planks. I lie around on my Army cot hoping the baby won't come too early. Hiroshi fashioned a crude wooden bench outside our "barracks" from an apple crate he found. Now I can get some fresh air, though there's not much sun because our place is located on the north side. I long for the walnut trees that waved along the sidewalk outside our store. Twisted barbed wire strands of fence with sharp, menacing points now replace my view. Instead of birds in the sky, I see guard towers with Army men pointing guns at our "homes." When I feel at my worst, I lament that we are being charged and imprisoned with the crime of having different shaped eyes. After all, I am as American as you are! I have made one friend who hardly even looks Japanese. When I asked about her heritage, she said she was only one-sixteenth! Every day I wonder how long we will be in this temporary "camp" and if "real" camps are being built.

Lolly, I truly want to believe in America, though as time passes by in this stable, I'm getting frantic with worry about bringing a baby into this type of place. I think about my store and wonder if the Soleskys are minding it. Then, I fret about my precious paintings that remain on the wall in my living room.

I may have left most of my possessions behind, but I do have my memories. Enclosed is a poem I wrote on the bus when Frankie was napping on Hiroshi's lap.

By the way, how is Fala? I miss his love and affection sorely, but I'm sure you're taking good care of him.

I think about you, your sweet daughter, and how much fun our boys had together. Frankie talks about Billy every day, even though he has many friends to play with here.

Please write back soon to cheer me up!
Your friend, Sumi

I closed my eyes a moment, overwhelmed with the picture of my friend in such a place. It wasn't that long ago that we'd had tea together. I opened her poem, and read:

Jeane Slone

Only What I Can Carry

Only what I can carry
Two suitcases
One for each hand

Will they fit?
My precious letters
My mother's jewelry
My *Hinamatsuri* doll collection
My family's photographs

Will there be space for...
My Japanese paintings
My mother's embroidered lamp
My father's oak rocking chair
My RCA phonograph

There is abundant room for...
My courage
My pride
My memories
But most of all, my dignity

The poem stunned me, stirring up frantic thoughts, making me feel helpless. I was quite shaken by thoughts of Sumi giving birth in a tiny horse stable. I had read that the Japanese were interned in nice camps and had pictured a resort-like atmosphere, not a smelly, cramped stall. Guilty feelings pricked me as I thought about leaving Fala alone all day. I folded the letter and was happy the lunch hour was almost over, glad to have my welding to distract me from my worrying frenzy.

The word *dignity* swirled inside my head. I was just about to clear my dishes from the table when a man sat down next to me.

"Hi Lolly. I see you got a job, though I'm not surprised; you were one of the best welders in my class," Mr. Cunningham said with a flirtatious wink.

"Hi, Mr. Cunningham. I'm welding on the SS *Red Oak.* Wha-what are you doing at the shipyard?" I stammered, feeling his eyes on me.

"I teach safety classes here." He flashed a broad smile.

The whistle blew a short blast. I grabbed my lunch. "I'd better go. Bye, Mr. Cunningham."

He raised his eyebrows. "Call me Phil."

I smiled and walked away thinking, He sure looks like Glenn Miller.

In a way, it made me feel wonderful to have such a smart man flirt with me.

On the way back to Shipyard #1, I wondered how Mr. Cunningham knew my nickname, when on all the papers in the class I had written Mrs. Lauretta O'Brien.

Chapter 14: My Husband

Exhausted but fulfilled from working at the shipyard, I decided to take a bus to the National Dollar Store instead of picking up the children right away. I had to find the right pants for Billy, fearing the wrath of Mrs. Ginzberg if I wasn't able to find any. After I found two pairs, I caught a bus that dropped me off right near the center.

I said hello to the receptionist, and with a cautious eye glanced about, relieved Mrs. Ginzberg was nowhere to be found. I placed the pants in a bag in Billy's small wooden square that I heard was called a "cubbyhole." I got in the line at the kitchen to get my dinner box to bring home before I found the children. Mrs. Ginzberg had told me to do it that way so the kids didn't have to wait with me and misbehave.

I washed the dishes that night, hung a load of laundry in the backyard, then got the children to bed. Exhausted, I plopped down on the sofa, eager to read a letter from Joe.

Dear Lolly:

I'm on the ship but can't tell you specifically where I am. I hope you are managing with the money I sent you. The $99 a month is not nearly as much as when I was working for the trucking company. I hope you'll do OK. I heard all the Japs are gone now and feel a lot better about leaving my family behind. I'm getting quite tired of the food on the ship and I especially miss your delicious chicken dinners. I've been at sea so many days, watching the sun set and rise, set and rise with no land in sight.

I sure miss you babe, and the kids.
Your loving husband, Joe
P.S. Why aren't you writing every day?

After reading the letter, dark thoughts crept upon me, reflecting on Joe's anger toward the Japanese-Americans. I couldn't imagine what he would say about Hattie!

Not all the good people in this world are Irish, I thought. I must try not to fall asleep after my nighttime chores and write back to him tomorrow night.

As I reread the letter, his love shone through this time. He did miss me and was concerned about the children. It cheerfully crossed my mind that maybe Joe would end up coming home on the ship I had been helping to build! I put the envelope on the table, and felt a bit regretful that I still hadn't gotten around to telling him about my new job. But after all, this was the only way I could supplement his paycheck.

I dragged myself to bed, and missed Joe's feel and smell of his manly body next to mine; his soothing, rhythmic snoring that used to rock me to sleep. I tossed and turned, and then thought I didn't miss how demanding he was in bed. At least I didn't have to worry every month about getting pregnant anymore. Edna and Billy were a handful enough for my short patience.

Chapter 15: Oodles of Friends

It was jumpin' in the break room during lunch hour the next day. A few of the gals lined up with their arms around each other and sang a new song, "Rosie the Riveter":

All day long whether rain or shine,

She's a part of the assembly line.

She's making history,

Working for victory

Hattie and I joined in on the refrain. The rest of the gals made the "BRRRR" riveting noise and tapped pencils on the bench. They finished up singing:

Keeps a sharp outlook for sabotage.

Sitting up there on the fuselage.

That little girl will do more than a male will do.

Everyone sang out "Rosie the Riveter!"

Ruby played a fake trumpet with her hands to her mouth, just like I heard the Four Vagabonds on the radio. She purred with her tongue the "BRRRR" noise.

We had a grand ole time. Work sure was more fun

than being cooped up at home all day. After we sang, Hattie and I settled down and ate our sandwiches.

"Do you live in Richmond?" I asked her.

"Yessum, I'm a boarder an' share a room with a married couple."

"You mean that you sleep with them?"

"Naw, we work opposite shifts, the beds are a'ways used an' warm, but I don't see 'em much, anyways."

"What about the weekend?"

"Saturday I sleep at Keva Theater on MacDonald, where my pal Polly sleeps. That way I give 'em some alone time, if ya'll know what I mean." She winked, then added, "Sundays I sleep on the floor."

I gasped, trying to picture this arrangement. "Your friend sleeps in a movie house?"

"Yes'um, she's been waitin' for a room to rent for almost a month now, but it's cheaper to sleep in the theater 'cause it's only 25 cents to get in. Why, it even costs $1.50 a night for a seat at the barber shop."

"I guess I don't know how good I have it."

"There are 'bout 19 theaters in town, and believe you me there's a lot a cheap sleepin' goin' on. Polly knows which ones are flea houses and which ones ain't. Why, most of the injuns workin' here sleep over on the other side of the tracks in box cars."

I packed up my lunch and shook my head as my mind filled with all of Hattie's tales. From the sidelines I noticed that a woman named Vera had been listening to our conversation the entire time. She was the only gal who did not join in with everyone's gay-making. I smiled at her, but

75

she avoided my friendliness and slipped out of the locker room.

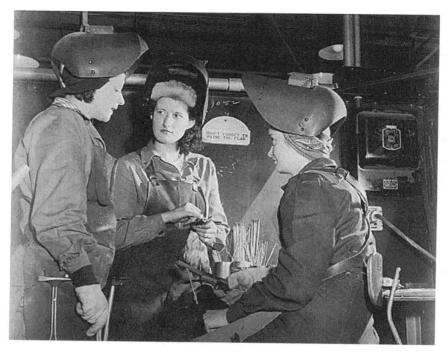

White women welders

I was quite fatigued from my long day at work, but pleased with all my accomplishments. It was very satisfying learning a new skill and finding great friends. I walked the several blocks to the Child Development Center. Upon entering, there were two policemen speaking to the director, holding the hand of a dirty-faced little waif about Edna's age.

"We have room for her to sleep upstairs, but I sure hope you find her mother. We are not an orphanage, you know." Mrs. Ginzberg shook a finger at the officers.

"That's our next task, Mrs. Ginzberg, to find the parent. Almost every day we find a child asleep in an automobile. Sometimes they're all groggy and we can only guess they've been given some kind of a pill to keep them asleep until their mother gets off her shift. We find children wandering around all hours of the day."

"Try to tell everyone you know there's a day care center now and an automobile is nowhere to leave a young child." She tapped with impatience on the counter.

"We're meeting with the head of the shipyard today for that reason."

"Here, give them this Office of Education leaflet. I don't mean to be cross, but it just makes me furious to think of children being left alone all day. Thanks for bringing her here." She lightly squeezed the child's hand.

"You're welcome. Good night, ma'am."

I saw the officers take the brochures and leave.

"Come here, darling. Let's get you into a proper bed," Mrs. Ginzberg said to the little girl. "Mrs. O'Brien, please meet me in my office. I need to take this child upstairs."

Nervously, I wondered whether she had gotten Billy's extra pants. Sitting in Mrs. Ginzberg's office, I read all her diplomas on the wall. Tired of waiting, I skimmed over the pamphlet from the pile on her desk that she had given the officers. *Good care for the children of working mothers means more planes and armaments for our fighting men, bringing victory to our Nation sooner.*

"Hello, Mrs. O'Brien. How are you this evening?" Mrs. Ginzberg said with her usual formal voice as she entered the office.

"Fine, thank you." I tried to speak slowly, but wanted

77

to get this meeting over with.

"I need to talk to you about Billy."

"I did bring his new pants today," I said, squirming and cracking my knuckles.

Mrs. Ginzberg glared at my hands. "Yes, thanks for bringing them. We didn't find the pants until later in the day. Billy keeps wetting himself. He missed going outside today because of his accidents. We had him wait for his pants to dry on the line. He's quite an intelligent little boy and participates well in the reading circle. But, I'm sorry to tell you that Billy's toilet troubles might be symptomatic of emotional disturbances. On the weekend you need to take him every hour to the toilet. If we're going to make any progress with his training, you must help us get the job done." She put her hand on her hip, waiting for my reply.

"Edna used the toilet easily," I mumbled.

"Girls seem to be easier, but that's no excuse to give up. As I said, you need to work on this when you get home every day," she lectured.

"I'll try harder." I frowned and looked out the doorway.

"Good. By the way, have him wash his hands after every toileting." She went through the pile of mail on her desk.

I rose and headed out the door, full of rejection, forcing myself to say, "Thanks, Mrs. Ginzberg."

The bus ride home was longer than usual. The children were full of conversation, but I was too exhausted to listen. I worried about what the director had said about Billy being emotionally disturbed. I should have listened to Sumi and tried the M&M method instead of eating them all myself. Mrs. Ginzberg did say he was smart during story time. I reassured myself with this thought as I redid Edna's braid. Edna chatted on and on about her day. When I felt my wet lap from Billy's behind, I knew I had a big job ahead of me.

Chapter 16: Flash Burn

Hattie and I worked quite well together when there was a piece of sheet metal that needed joining. She welded one side while I equally welded the other; that way it didn't buckle. We did an excellent job connecting all the pieces. The gear we had to wear—the hood, over-sized gloves, and leather jacket—was very heavy and uncomfortable. The next piece we had ahead of us measured about 40-50 feet long. It was a good thing the sheets were in the right place, as they were very heavy, and we would not have been able to move them. After I found the right number welding rod, I nodded my trusty hood down and put the rod into the electric stinger. I made a beautiful line of liquid flux beadwork, bringing back a memory of my mother embroidering the edging of a tablecloth. I made a pass with the rod, then a second, well-designed one. The stinger produced flying fireworks of cobalt and sparkling gold. The sizzling noise reminded me of a thick, juicy steak frying on the stove.

Hattie finished her line as I finished mine. I flipped my hood up as we each chipped the slag with a hammer and brushed it smooth with a wire brush. Then we went on to the next piece. I put in a different size rod this time, nodded my hood down with pride, and watched the liquid turn into tiny jewel-like beads. With the welded line finished, I jerked my neck up to move my welding hood so I could wipe the sweat off my nose. Suddenly, a streak of glowing blue light hit the sides of my eyes. A sudden flash had appeared from Hattie's stinger. I panicked and grabbed my hood down, unable to see. Moving backwards, I felt the wall with my jacket and slid down to sit on the floor to wait for my sight to come back. As I sat there, I listened to all the noise of the workers around me. When I felt better, I got up and continued on with my welding. As Hattie finished, I placed my welding hood up with caution, looked around, stood up and proceeded to chip the slag with my hammer, then brushed it shiny smooth.

Toward the end of the day, I knew I hadn't escaped the flash burn from Hattie's stinger. I got my lunch box from my locker and suddenly let out a deep, guttural moan.

"What's wrong, honey chile?" Hattie rushed over to me.

Between short gulps of air I yelled, "I think I got a flash burn, my eyeballs feel like razor blades are slicing them!"

Hattie held onto my elbow, guiding me to a bench. "Here, set yourself down. I'll fetch the foreman." She flew out of the room.

It felt like hours as I sat grinding my teeth in pain, then I heard a crack and screamed, "Oh my God, I broke a tooth!"

I felt the foreman dab a dribble of blood that ran down the corner of my mouth. He yelled at me with fury, "Stop grindin' yer teeth! Close yer eyes an' hold on to my arm. Walk as fast as ya can to the jeep. I'll drive you to Kaiser Hospital. If ya weren't a dame I'd tell ya to lay down, put a sliced potato on 'em and just ride it out."

My eyes stung worse after I shut them. I heard Hattie say, "I'll come."

The foreman grunted, "Nigger, I don't need you!"

I panted and moaned as he fiercely grabbed my arm,

dragging me up the metal stairs. Cursing at my noises, he spat, "Oh, shut up. That's what ya get for not keeping yer hood down. Now you'll remember!" He snickered, grabbing my elbow tighter.

Several flights later I could feel the cool air on my face and knew we were on the top deck.

"Would ya move faster?" he snarled. Pushing me roughly into a jeep, we sped off, the open air relieving the pain ever so slightly.

On the ride to the hospital, I was subjected to a barrage of derogatory remarks from the uncouth foreman. "Lady, I got some free advice for ya. That zigaboo you're friends with is just an advanced animal beast. Back where I come from we'd string a nigger up every now and then just to keep the rest of them in order. You best stay away from them and stick to your own kind."

I shivered in the seat and kept my thoughts to myself.

I rested on a cot in the hospital with a wet cloth on my eyes. The pills the nurse gave me helped reduce the pain a bit. I began to fret about Billy and Edna. "Nurse, nurse, I need to get my children at the center!" I yelled out into the darkness.

"You are aren't going anywhere, dear."

"But, my children..."

"Where are they?"

"At the Maritime Child Development Center." I rubbed my eyes.

"I'll telephone over there and see what can be done. Now, miss, if you don't leave your eyes alone, I'll have to tie your hands down. Try to rest until the medication does its job and puts you to sleep."

"Billy, Edna," I moaned, drifting off through the throbbing pain.

Negro women welders

Chapter 17: The Safety Instructor

The following week our first safety class was held and I got the opportunity to watch and listen to Mr. Cunningham. He was quite a hunk.

"So far, our Kaiser Hospital treats an average of 500 cases a day. This includes eye injuries, bruises, and broken bones. By the way, class, don't forget to take your salt tablets, they're available at every drinking fountain on the ship. The salt replaces what is lost in your body through perspiration on the job. We've already had over twenty employees die at work from dehydration," Mr. Cunningham lectured, pointing at figures on the chalkboard. "I'd like to discuss flash burns and how to prevent them. I'm sure you all know to keep your hoods down so you won't get flash burns when you're welding, but it's just as important not to put your hood up too fast when you're around other welders, also."

"What's flash burn like?" Rosa asked.

"Mrs. O'Brien, would you mind telling us about your experience with flash burns? I've gotten some, but it was a long time ago. The class could benefit if you wouldn't mind telling us about the recent accident you had." Mr. Cunningham looked straight at me.

I blushed, then felt the sharp triangle from my broken tooth. I described to the class my painful flash burn and how it had occurred. "The nurse at the hospital told me the flash burn I got from being exposed to someone's welding is called 'arc eye.' It happens when the cornea, which she said is the transparent front of the eye that covers the iris and pupil, is exposed to the ultraviolet light in welding. I had to stay in the hospital for two days with dressings that covered my eyes. The doctor checked them periodically to make sure they did not become infected. He said that an infection could lead to loss of vision."

Mr. Cunningham said, "Thanks for that excellent description, Mrs. O'Brien. It's similar to getting a sunburn. You don't feel it until later on. Remember everyone, keep your collars buttoned up to protect yourselves from the spark, so there's no exposed skin. Also, put your gloves on tight; that way the sparks can't fly down the cuffs."

He was such an intelligent, kind man, I thought, compared to the nasty foreman who had rushed me to the hospital.

The teacher continued his discourse. "The safety commission has decided women should not be wearing jewelry of any kind, including wedding rings, when they're at work."

Many of the gals groaned after that announcement. Vera sat with her long legs stretched out and spent most of the class examining the ceiling or corners of the room, avoiding any eye contact.

Before the lunch break I asked Hattie her feelings about being called a "nigger."

"Oh, it don't bother me none. I'm used to it. I was called more than that in Alabama." She smiled a wide smile, showing all her teeth—and she seemed to have so many!

I had allowed myself the extravagance of going to the canteen once a week. When I invited Hattie, she said she had to send all her extra money home to her mama. The sound and feel of the jingling coins in my deep pocket was very satisfying. I loved earning my own paycheck.

While I read the lunch sign, "Welders Special," I saw Mr. Cunningham out of the corner of my eye. I quickly ordered, and with food in hand, I headed to the far end of the canteen away from him.

I heard him call out my name."Hey, Lolly, sit here."

My heart gave a little jump, making me smile. The only spot available was right next to him. I hesitated as he moved toward the end more and patted the bench.

"How are you doing?" His eyes fell on mine.

"Fine, Mr. Cunningham." I fiddled with my wedding ring and then gazed at his clean, well-pressed work shirt. He was a much smaller man than my Joe, but his open, welcome face warmed my insides.

"You've known me long enough now to call me Phil." He offered me his apple.

"No thanks, uh, Phil." I shoved in a bite of my salami sandwich and glanced over at his left hand, noticing that he didn't have a wedding band. Maybe he didn't wear one because of work.

I guess I should start leaving mine at home, I thought.

"Did you hear about MacArthur's return? Over 600 ships have been sent to the Philippines to wipe out the rest of the Japanese." He waved his arms about energetically.

I smiled slightly. I didn't want to talk about the war. It only reminded me of my Joe, and I surely didn't want to be a widow with two small children.

Phil changed the subject. "There's a grand movie playing at the Keva Theater. I'd love to take you there."

"I couldn't. I've got two kids to pick up at the day care center every night." For some reason I failed to mention the fact that I was also married.

"Do they have night care there?"

"They did stay over a night once when I had my accident."

"Why don't you tell the day care you have to work overtime and take in a show with me?" Phil persisted.

"Well, um, you know, umm, Mr., uh, I mean Phil, I am married," I stammered.

"I assumed that, Lolly, but I'm not! I also figured your husband's in the service. It's just a movie, there's nothing wrong with going out with a friend." He tilted his glasses and grinned at me.

"I suppose. I haven't been to a picture show in a very long time."

"Great" he gushed. "I'll meet you right here Tuesday after work."

Mr. Cunningham took off before I could protest.

Chapter 18: Tuskegee Airmen

After seeking out Mrs. Ginzberg that morning at the Child Care Center, I nervously attempted small talk. "How's everything going at the center, Mrs. Ginzberg? There are so many new students here."

"We get more and more working mothers enrolling their children all the time. There are ten centers in Richmond alone, operated by the Board of Education and financed by the federal government with over a thousand children being cared for every day. Your Kaiser Shipyard sponsors this one." A proud smile spread on her face.

"I'm not surprised there are that many with the war continuing to rage on. There appears to be fewer men at work and more working gals." Trying to impress her I added, "It seems like child care is becoming a wartime necessity, despite reading that FBI director Mr. Hoover said, 'Mothers already have war jobs at home.'"

"If we're to win this war, we must all do our part. I think we'll see the light at the end of the tunnel soon," the director remarked with a positive note.

"I hope," I said as I thought about my Joe at sea. "Mrs. Ginzberg, I was asked to work overtime tomorrow. Can the children spend the night?" I tried to say this sincerely, hoping my lie wouldn't shine through.

"Of course, it's very patriotic of you to work so much. This is why we have night care. Make sure you bring extra soakers for Billy, just in case."

"I will, thanks," I blushed.

As we walked with Billy toward his classroom, Mrs. Ginzberg seemed to notice my change in color and said with reassurance, "Billy's toileting is coming along. You must be practicing at home."

"I have." I inwardly smiled, happy I had purchased a tube of M&M's when I bought the new pants for Billy.

Billy ran into his classroom, went up to an easel, and very carefully painted large blue circles.

"Bye, Billy. Those are nice circles. Have fun today!"

Billy placed the brush in the bottle, came after me, hugged my legs and said, "Love you!"

I scooped him up, twirled him around, kissed his sweet, sweet cheeks several times, and said goodbye.

At work when the noon whistle blew, Hattie and I climbed up the stairs toward the break room. Hattie got out her lunch as I poured my soup into my metal thermos cup. There was Vera again, sitting in the far corner with no lunch in sight.

"Did you hear the joke about the hillbillies from Tennessee?" Vera suddenly announced to everyone in the locker room. This question caused complete stillness in the bustling room.

A girl named Roslyn eyed Vera suspiciously. "I'm from Tennessee."

Smirking, Vera continued, "They thought the toilet

was to wash their feet in!" She slapped her pants and laughed loudly. No one else joined in.

I broke the silence in the room. "Where are you from, Hattie?"

"I'm from Alabama, ma'am."

"You know, you don't have to call me *ma'am*. It makes me feel uncomfortable." I unbuttoned my welder's jacket and noticed that her face was baby-smooth, like polished mahogany.

"Yes um, Lolly, I'm sure glad not to be in Alabama where I have to call the White people Miss or Mrs. I came here on the Southern Pacific rail with my bruther after my husband joined the Army. At the beginnin' stretch of my trip all the coloreds sat behind a black curtain on a long bench. When we switched trains in the West, we were taken aback to see a colored sittin' right next to a White!"

"I've never been out of this state and don't know much about the South." My eyes grew wide.

"Before I left, a family friend, a colored nurse, went in front of the Whites to get on the bus, an she was beaten an jailed!" Hattie shook her head sadly.

"How horrible!"

"I got tired of cookin', washin', and ironin' for Mrs. Jenkins. Why, I barely was given enough money to rub two nickels together. Count your blessin' you've never been to Alabama. I feel free as a dog without a leash livin' here with white folks treatin' me like their equal." Hattie munched down her sandwich.

"When I was little and saw a Negro person for the first time, I asked my mom why he was that color. She told me, 'Makes no difference, we're all the same color inside.'" I finished my orange and put my lunchbox in my locker.

"True 'nough!" Hattie searched around in her bag. "Wonder where my candy bar went to? I could'da sworn I put it in there this mornin'."

"My husband's on a ship in the Pacific, where's yours stationed?" I asked and watched her rummage around.

"My husband's a pilot at the Tuskegee air base in Alabama. My bruther's in the Navy. He's stationed right here 'cross the bay at Port Chicaga."

"I wish my Joe was that close."

"Me sittin' talkin' to you, Lord a mercy, this would've never happened in the South." Hattie shook her head, and re-knotted her kerchief in the front as her big, gold hoop earrings jingled about.

On the other side of the break room, Hazel, Ruby, and Roslyn got up and spontaneously began to sing "We're the Janes Who Make the Planes."

We're the Janes who make the planes and we're givin' ev'ry fightin' man a chance.

We're the girls who clipped our curls and from now on we're the ones who wear the pants!

Sweetheart in overalls with a smudge on her chin, and a victory grin.

Proudly helping them to win, over there!

Someday she'll settle down, and put on her gingham gown, when it's all over.

Another gal broke out her harmonica, adding to the tune. Hattie and I joined right in clapping. The singing loosened up my sore shoulders and back. Even though welding physically exhausted me, I wouldn't trade it now for being home all day with no one to talk to.

When our shift was almost over, Hattie got out a letter from her locker. "Can you help me, um, read this? My hubby's a ed-u-cated man. I only made it to the second grade, then had to work after daddy died to help mama support my eight bruthers an' sisters."

"Sure, I'd love to." I read the letter out loud:

To my Sweetie Pie:

I miss and dream about you every night, wanting your soft body wrapped around mine.

My Army buddies and I have been working extra hard here at the Tuskegee Air Base. We know we are called an experiment, and are competing fiercely against the Whites to prove our value, even though most of us are college educated and highly qualified. We are trying to prove to them that our brains are not smaller than theirs and we are just as capable as they are when it comes to flying.

In the other branches of the service, our people end up serving as janitors or work in kitchens and don't get to fight for our country.

My buddies and I talk about experiencing a double war; we have to fight for our race as well as our country. Most of the guys say "Let's win the double victory!" Victory over our enemies from without, and second victory over our enemies within. I'm ready to serve my country during a time when our nation has its greatest emergency, but why can't we be in a mixed regiment and put all racial discrimination aside?

Yancey Williams is in my squadron, and he is quite famous here. He filed a lawsuit to force the U.S. government to let him join the Army Air Corps. Thanks to him, the day after his court appearance Negro pilots were accepted in the service!

On the trip here, my buddies told me they all sat together even though it was not a segregated train. At one of the stops a White lieutenant ordered them to stand and give their seats to Italian prisoners of war. The lieutenant even made two female Negro WAACs give up their seats!

New training facilities had to be built here, so the Whites wouldn't have to share runways with us. I just have one week left of this grueling five-week flight training to earn my silver wings. I hope you got a job and your brother is watching after you for me. Sorry this letter is short, I'll have more time later to write.

Love, your Granger

P.S. Why haven't you written to me? I have written two letters to you and have received none. I miss you so!

I handed Hattie the letter and gave her a suspicious sideways glance as I approached a delicate subject. "It sounds like you have quite a wonderful husband."

Hattie's eyes lit up, her eyelashes fluttering. "Yes'um, I love'um with all my heart an' soul."

"I have an extra V-mail that you could write him back on. By the way, in case you don't know what V-mail is, it is a letter photographed onto microfilm. They say one reel can hold 18,000 letters and saves the needed shipping space for war equipment.""

"Why, thank ya kindly, I'll let ya know if I need it." Hattie fiddled with the hood on her welding helmet that lay on the bench.

Finally, I asked her if her husband knew that she couldn't write. She averted her eyes down to her lap.

I broke the silence. "I'll write it for you."

She burst out, "That'll be swell!"

"I'll bring a V-mail to work tomorrow and we'll write a letter made in heaven to that marvelous husband of yours."

"Why, bless your heart. I can't thank ya enough." Her smile pushed her shiny teeth out.

"It's nothing. It would make me feel like I'm doing my bit for the war and your husband has a big part in it by being a pilot. How did you pass the written part on the welding test?"

"Can ya'll keep a secret?"

"Of course!"

"Mr. Cunningham ask'd me the questions after class one day."

"You sure seem smart enough to learn to read and write." I patted her lap with reassurance.

"I'll learn someday, maybe when this war's over and I git to settle down with mah sweetie."

Later, when I lifted my favorite strawberry colored church dress with the flared skirt over my head, a quiet whistle from out of nowhere floated through the air. I turned around and there was Vera, giving me the onceover.

Hattie said, "Mah, mah, looks like you're off to do the town up."

I smiled, felt a ragged nail, and said, "I'm just going to catch a picture show with a friend."

"Well, ya'll have a gay ole time now, ya hear?" Hattie gave me a beautiful, wide-mouthed grin.

I anxiously applied mascara in the bathroom and it smeared in the corner of my eye. Rubbing the excess off turned my eyeball red. I jammed my makeup kit in my purse, wondering what in the world I was doing.

Tuskegee Airman

Chapter 19: Toyo, a Japanese Friend

I met Phil at the canteen. He was wearing a stylish two-button suit with a vest. His oxfords looked new, but I figured they most likely were well kept since it was almost impossible to buy shoes that weren't for work these days. He looked very handsome and intelligent.

"You look...wow, Lolly!"

"Thanks," I blushed.

"My car's parked across the yard." He held my elbow and guided me there.

"I haven't been in a car since Daddy died. Your Model A reminds me of him," I chatted nervously as I faced the highly polished automobile.

"We're going to see *Casablanca*. A friend of mine told me it's a swell movie full of wartime patriotism. My favorite!" Phil opened the car door for me.

"My sister wrote me about it." My tension eased as I smoothed my dress under, slid onto the seat of the well-cleaned automobile and thought of how messy Joe's truck always was.

Phil got into the car on the other side. "Where does she live?" he asked, turning the ignition.

"She moved to New York with her husband because he got a job transfer. After the bombing of Pearl Harbor, he joined the Army, then Diana got a job riveting airplanes."

"That's wonderful. We can use all the workers we can get to win this war, and women sure have proven to be just what we need!" He moved his eyes from the road flirtatiously toward mine. "How's work been?"

"I enjoy all the gals. When we're not hard at welding, we're singing in the locker room during break time. Most of the men are rude, though."

"I know what you mean. There's the seamy side of working on a ship. I've seen wise guys smashing light bulbs with rocks, lighting their cigarettes with torches and burning their names with them, wasting metal. Many of them throw their leftover lunch overboard."

"Yeah," I nodded, and added, "I've seen men in corners playing craps during work. One of them saw me watching and coughed, then spat a gob on my cheek!"

Phil added heatedly, "I've caught guys going over the fence to nearby bars for drinks during work hours. It's downright disgraceful all the loafing going on sometimes, but all in all, we pretty much have very dedicated crew."

To test his personality, I mentioned Sumi, curious about Phil's opinion on Japanese-Americans.

"Horse stables? How dreadful! I thought they were in barracks like the Army soldiers. Wonder how my friend Tom is."

"Who's Tom?" My mind filled with questions.

"His real name is Toyo. He's a Japanese-American, Nisei, born here. I used to weld with him before Pearl Harbor and he was a darn good welder! Right after the bombing, he came to work but couldn't find his time card and asked me about it. The foreman came over and said there was no longer any work for him."

"That was obviously a bunch of malarkey." I unconsciously repeated something Joe always said.

"I saw him in town. He told me about the evacuation, madly saying he was as American as I was."

My mind raced with thoughts of Sumi, hoping she was doing all right.

Phil anxiously continued, "I read in the newspaper Tom got plastic surgery on his eyelids, changed his name, then got arrested in San Leandro after someone reported a 'Jap' on the street."

"He did all that?" My hands pressed in my lap.

"The newspaper quoted him as saying, 'I was born here, send me into the Army, but I'm not going to some internment prison camp.'"

"God knows we need as many troops as possible." Now I was upset and I bit my teeth together.

Phil drove slower and continued, "The newspaper said the director of the American Civil Liberties Union wanted to use his case to test the legality of the Japanese-American internment. The director paid the outrageous bail, but Tom was taken to Tanforan because his trial wasn't until September. He's writing to me as a friend since he's been rejected by his own people at the camp because of his actions."

"It's swell of you to correspond with him." I smiled, thinking of Sumi once again.

"He was a damned good welder."

Phil turned into a parking space at the Keva Theater and shut off the engine. When he touched my arm to help me out, I moved it anxiously away.

Chapter 20: The Picture Show

We watched a newsreel short titled *The Glamour Girls*. It showed women working in factories inspecting parachutes, going through machine parts on an assembly line, and driving buses.

The lively narrator stated, "There are over 300,000 women who work in the aircraft industry now, but there are still not enough workers. They are being added as fast as they apply. Married women are signing up, knowing this is a short-time emergency situation just for the duration of the war. Working in a factory is no more difficult than house-work. Instead of cutting the lines of a dress, this woman cuts the pattern of aircraft parts. Instead of baking a cake, she is cooking gears to reduce the tension of the parts after use. Just with a short apprenticeship, this woman can operate a drill press just as easily as a juice extractor in her own kitchen. When necessary, machinery is adapted for feminine muscles, like this lazy-arm drill to take the strain off. Women can do jobs as well as men and get the same pay. Gals, longing won't bring him back sooner... Get a War Job! See your United States Employment Service now!"

We settled into our seats as the main attraction, *Casablanca*, came on. The Negro piano player had a terrific voice and style when he sang, "It's Got to Be You." My foot tapped along with the melody. Phil's shoe bumped into mine as he tapped, too.

From the corner of my eye, I saw him creep his arm around the back of my chair, sneaking his fingers to rest upon my shoulder. I stiffened during the song "As Time Goes By," especially when they sang, "A kiss is just a kiss..." The word "kiss" brought sinful thoughts swimming in my head. It made me wonder, What am I doing in a movie theater with another man? A picture of Joe being shot at flashed through my mind as I ate a huge handful of popcorn.

Phil gazed at me with his charming smile and drummed on my arm during another song. The piano music was heaven-sent.

The end of the movie caught me wiping a tear away. When the lights came on, Phil gave me a comforting smile, placed his handkerchief in my lap, and said, "That was some movie!"

"It was as good as my sister said it would be." With care I wiped my eyes so the mascara wouldn't run. Joe would have hated the movie because of all the romance...not that we ever went to the show.

In the lobby Phil bought a war bond and winked at me. "For the war effort." He pinned the "*Buy Bonds*" button on my coat. I glanced longingly at next week's poster showing the movie *Swing Shift Maisie,* starring Ann Sothern and James Craig.

The winter air was still and calm, like the ride home.

Phil broke the silence. "It's too bad Ilsa was already married, because I think they would've been a great couple, don't you?" He made a smooth right turn onto Cutting Boulevard.

"She did love her husband, but not with as much compassion as she did Rick. I admire her commitment to her husband, though." We passed my pale brown house and I giggled nervously. "That was my house on the corner."

Phil turned around, then parked the car. He faced me. "They had that unbeatable chemistry between them that some people say happens only once in a lifetime."

"I felt their magnetism, but the hidden message in the movie rang true for me. Sacrifices must be made and wartime causes great sacrifices." My feelings squirmed about, causing a hot flush upon my face. I reached for the door handle.

Phil jumped out and opened the door for me. We strolled toward the house, then up the porch steps.

He kissed me on the cheek. "I had a swell time. Thanks for keeping me company."

Before I could agree, he was down the steps and driving off into the distance, leaving me with a mixture of want and relentless guilt.

When I opened the door, Fala greeted me, doing his happy dance, then sat and cocked his head, making me feel uncomfortable. His doggy face seemed to say, "What have you been up to and where are Billy and Edna?"

Chapter 21: Broken Legs

The children were quite demanding that weekend. I tried to have them help me with all the household chores that had piled up from the workweek. All the busyness kept my mind from my shameful encounter with Phil.

I canned a chicken to send to Joe. Edna helped me make Tollhouse cookies to send, as well. Billy ate some of the popcorn I used as a packaging cushion for the care package. I saved the chicken broth for my work thermos. The fats were put aside to bring to the butcher shop to be sent for making glycerin in explosives. "Waste not, want not," I said to the children, even though they didn't understand. I thought, Food is a weapon; don't waste it! Joe would have heartily agreed with that new slogan.

At dinner Edna surprised me with a prayer she learned from the center. "God is great, God is good, let us thank Him for this food."

After her prayer, I thought, Thank you, God, for Billy not wetting himself all weekend!

After the kids were in bed, I unfolded a letter from Diana. Unbuckling my old heels, I lay on the davenport in my ankle socks and read:

Dear Lolly:

I have plenty of time to write to you now because I am lying in bed with two broken legs! I was on the aileron lettering

103

the side of the airplane with Army numbers when some smart-alec came along and moved my ladder. I fell ten feet to the concrete. Nobody could prove Butch shoved it aside, but then, no one was around. As I was being taken away on the stretcher I heard the boys saying, "She must've missed a step, somethin' I would never do!" Just before that incident, during break time the gals and I were discussing how to handle these nasty boys. We figure they are mean because of getting rejected when they tried to join the service, so they take their anger out on us.

A few of the gals came by and brought me some flowers and now we're all going to watch out for each other very carefully. We've found the only way to gain respect is to outperform the men; we never had to "look busy" at home! I'll write more tomorrow as I'm getting very tired.

Love, Diana

P.S. Now that I have time, I'm reading Thomas Wolfe's You Can't Go Home Again. *I find it fascinating that the hero is madly in love with a married woman. Makes for a juicy story!*

My God, I hope her legs will recover, I thought. I could relate to what she meant by nasty boys at work, and missed all the long girl chats we used to have when she lived nearby. After I got undressed, I fell asleep and dreamed Phil was married and cheated on his wife by being with me. The dream woke me up as I felt the imprint of his kiss on my cheek.

Women airplane mechanics

Chapter 22: Port Chicago Explosion

I opened my locker, and after searching through it twice, I asked Hattie, "Have you seen my lunchbox?"

"No ma'am. I mean, Lolly."

"Where could it be? It was in my locker this morning."

"I heard Roslyn tellin' Ruby that her makeup kit is missin'."

"I'll be damned! There must be a thief around here, but everyone seems so sweet!"

"I sure like all the gals. I wonder if that's why I was missin' my candy bar a few weeks back?" Hattie fastened her locker tighter. "I won't be at work tomorra."

"Why's that?"

"I hafta go visit my bruther in the hospital."

"What happened?"

"An accident. He was doin' his job a loadin' munitions and a terrible explosion happened."

"Golly, was he hurt?"

"His buddy came by last night, tellin' me 'bout the explosion and that Sam was in the hospital. That's all he said."

On the way to the center to pick up the kids, I bought the *Chronicle* bearing the headline **Port Chicago Explosion**. I sat on the curb and eagerly read it.

At the Port Chicago Naval Base on Suisun Bay, 320 men died at a munitions shipment facility. There were 390 civilians and military personnel injured.

Munitions were being loaded by hand, crane, and winch aboard the cargo vessel bound for the Pacific Theater. Cargo included bombs, shells, naval mines, and torpedoes. After four days of around-the-clock loading of 4,600 tons of explosives, the ships were 40% full by that evening. Sixteen rail cars still held munitions waiting to be loaded before the explosion occurred.

The SS EA Bryan was detonated, causing a huge fireball three miles in diameter. The maiden SS Quinault Victory Ship, that recently had been delivered from the Kaiser shipyards, was torn into sections and thrown in several directions. The stern landed upside down in the water 500 feet away from the dock. The SS Quinault Victory contained a partial load of fuel oil.

The stevedores loading the ships were killed instantly.

A Coast Guard fireboat was thrown 600 feet upriver, where it sank. Chunks of glowing hot metal and burning ordnance were flung over 12,000 feet in the air.

The port's barracks and other buildings in the surrounding town were severely damaged. The shattered glass and a rain of jagged metal caused many additional injuries among both military and civilian populations. No one outside the immediate pier area was killed.

The explosion was so loud it was heard in a theater in Berkeley and broke windows at the Fairmont Hotel in San Francisco.

The body parts of the seaman littered the bay and port.

At first it was thought that the Japanese were attacking.

The cause of the explosion has not been determined, but there were implications that the sailors did not handle the ordnance correctly.

I folded the newspaper and whispered a prayer for Hattie's brother, then wondered if he would recover from the horrific accident.

Stevedores loading munitions

Permission from the National Park Service from the collection of
Port Chicago Naval Magazine National Memorial

Naval barracks after the explosion

Permission from the National Park Service from the collection of
Port Chicago Naval Magazine National Memorial

After the explosion, Port Chicago

Permission from the National Park Service from the collection of
Port Chicago Naval Magazine National Memorial

Chapter 23: The Launching

My heavy boots made a cheerful clanking noise as I climbed up the narrow metal staircase to the main deck. The ship was beginning to shape up and I felt a sense of pride knowing I helped build this magnificent vessel. It was lunch hour. Too bad Hattie was missing an entertainment day on the ship.

The Coast Guard band played the "Star Spangled Banner," then a new all-American girls band took over singing "Boogie Woogie Bugle Boy." Did they ever belt it out, swingin', swayin' and marchin' with their flashy red and white striped blouses and deep blue skirts. I tapped out the rhythm on my pants. There were two fellas in front of me. One was heavy set and the other a string bean with a wrinkly face. They loudly complained to each other.

"I'll tell ya right now, I don't like these girl bands. Girls need to leave this business to people who know what it's all about, and I mean men!" the skinny one said.

The fat one agreed. "Dame musicians are too emotional to play a decent set. Their facial contortions on the horn make 'em look like idiots!"

I tried to move toward a group of women who pointed at a man wearing a long, beautiful white robe who stood beside a captain.

"That's Prince Faisal of Saudi Arabia touring the ship," one of the women yelled.

The girl band ended with a catchy new song, "Pistol

112

Packin' Mama." Enthusiasm overcame me as I shouted out, "Hot Dog!"

This caused the fat fella to step back on my foot, rudely saying, "Watch where ya put your feet, lady. Ship buildin' ain't no place for a broad, anyway!"

I hobbled away from them. My tears surfaced as my foot throbbed. I fretted and wondered, Do I have to tell them how to behave? Don't they have sisters or mothers? I heard Ruby say all the nice young men had left and now we just had 4F old goats to bother us.

Boris Karloff came to the microphone, which distracted me from my pain. He appeared incredibly frightening, just like on the theater screen. I was surprised by what a soft-spoken, charming man he sounded like in person.

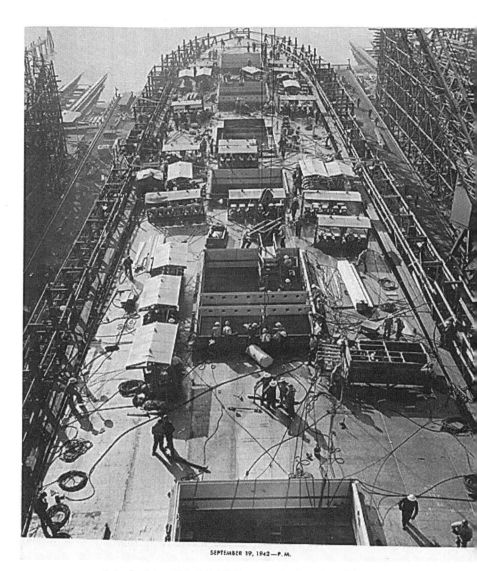

SEPTEMBER 19, 1942—P. M.

Marinship, CA 9/19/42, completing the ship

That night at the center, full of hesitation, I asked, "Mrs. Ginzberg, how's Billy doing?"

"I think we've made it over the hill, Mrs. O'Brien. He's fully toilet trained now." A proud expression formed on her face as she straightened a wrinkle on her well-ironed blouse.

Relief filled my voice. "I was hoping you'd say that. I've had no problems at home." Sumi's M&M trick had really worked. "I've been wondering, Mrs. Ginzberg, why doesn't Edna eat the oatmeal? She loves mine at home."

With an overly pleasant voice she responded, "We add cod liver oil. It may have a displeasing taste, but it combats rickets for some of our malnourished children. Please excuse me, I must do the dormitory count for the night. Have a good evening, Mrs. O'Brien."

When I went into Billy's classroom, a teacher was playing the piano and singing, "My Country 'Tis of Thee." Billy sat cross-legged next to Peter and, much to my surprise, sang most of the words.

In Edna's room, I saw her playing ring-around-the-rosie with the other girls. I overheard the head teacher talking to a new teacher. "It's very important not to play music during rest time. The children need to learn to relax without this help. Besides, the constant association of drowsiness with music may foster opera audience somnolence later in life." She made this statement in a high, snooty voice, sounding just like Mrs. Ginzberg.

This school was full of surprises. I learned something new every day in the short time I was there.

After Billy and Edna were tucked in bed, I carefully ironed a few of their clothes for the week, then lay on the sofa reading a letter from Sumi.

My dear friend Lolly:

It cheered me up to receive your letter about your welding job, but I can tell you are extremely worried about me. I'm happy to say there is progress happening here. A library opened with 65 books, and you know how much I like to read! I even got a children's picture book to look at with Franklin. Last week we got to see our first movie in the racetrack grandstand. It was called Spring Parade *with the beautiful movie star Deanna Durbin.*

We wonder, with all the new buildings that keep being built (like another mess hall), if we are really going to be relocated. Yesterday, there were lines of over 5,000 people waiting to be served a meal of Vienna sausages, two slices of bread, and a pitcher of tea for dinner. This was a special treat after we protested when liver was served three nights in a row. Before that it was beans and butterless bread. At first everyone was constantly hungry, now there is more food and many sinks for us to wash our individual dishes that were brought from home. We all do our part for Uncle Sam by cleaning and pressing any cans after meals.

The baby is due any day now. Though he or she will live with us in the horse stable, I'd rather have the baby here before moving again. Maybe a family of four sounds crowded in a 20 x 9 foot stall that is divided into two rooms, but next to us there is actually a family of six!

It's easy to count your blessings when you see other people who have it harder than you.

Seiko, who I have become fast friends with, sold her 26-room hotel for only $500.00. She hid the money in a bar of soap since all our bank accounts were frozen and we could only withdraw $100 before coming here. Her five-year-old daughter

116

broke out from the measles. A nurse came and took her away to keep the infection from spreading. Poor Seiko didn't see her for three weeks! This is what I mean by counting my blessings.

Please write as often as possible, it cheers me up to hear from you.

Your friend, Sumi

P.S. Enclosed is one of the drawings I made to keep my mind off waiting for the baby.

There was a second page to the letter. I unfolded it and saw a detailed, hand-inked drawing of Hiroshi with scissors cutting long grass growing between the planks on the horse stable floor. Even though her letter was a positive one, the drawing told me the true story. At the bottom of it she wrote, *The warping of the new lumber left cracks in the floor half an inch to an inch wide. Through the cracks the tall grass came up.*

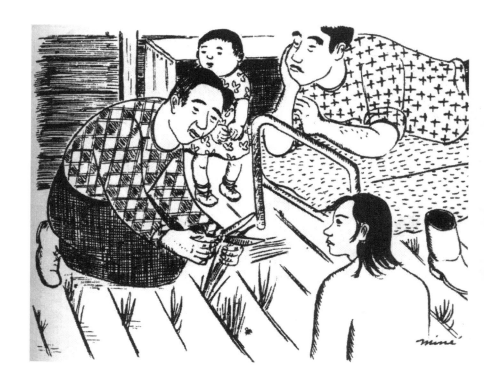

Drawing by Mine Okubo, Tanforan horse stable, 1942
San Bruno, CA. Courtesy Seiko Buckingham

Chapter 24: Freeman Field Mutiny

A few days later at work, I ached for an intelligent conversation. I went through the crowds trying to find Phil. Ignoring the catcalls, I thought, These so-called men just make women feel like outsiders, that working is a man's exclusive empire! I am tired of their razzing!

One creepy-looking fella bumped right into my breasts. I yelled, "Stop!"

He smirked and shrugged his shoulders. "Sorry, lady."

Roslyn told me to whistle and hoot back louder to astonish them, or throw them a cool "Thank you!" I wanted to plead with these 4F pigs to please keep their hands to themselves. Women are not just something entertaining to go to bed with! Mabel called them all schoolboys with bathroom jokes. All of them kept trying to unpeel our welder's duds with their eyes. I never knew how to react.

After I bought the special of the day from the sweet Chinese man, I carried it to a bench in the lunchroom. Hearing a soft whistle, I glanced up. Across the room I saw Phil waving at me. He was weaving his way through all the people. My heart quickened as I remembered his kiss.

I enjoyed listening to Phil's small talk about welding. It relaxed me.

"It's so hot when you're welding, and that's because the equipment reaches up to 6,500 degrees," he said.

"Gosh, no wonder my face gets so darn drippin' wet. I love making small pools of beads. I fashion them nice and even, just like when I used to embroider."

"That's why you're such a top welder, because you strive for perfection." He reached over and held my hand. "This wartime urgency for speed causes too many shortcuts. Haste makes waste. I get reports of foreign bodies in eyes, even foot lacerations from not wearing work boots. The head foreman told me violators of the safety rules will be dismissed, but the rush continues on."

I listened with rapt attention, enjoying all his facial expressions and gestures.

"There's a dance Friday night. I haven't cut a rug in quite a while. Let's go, Lolly."

"You know I'm married," I reminded him.

"But how can you dance with your husband when he's away on duty? I bet you're a swell dancer!" His eyes were all over me.

"I suppose I could say I'm needed for overtime again." My body flushed with desire.

Fully encouraged, he caressed my shoulder. "Meet me at the canteen at 7:00, Friday."

Before I could protest he took off. I sat there, my once warm body chilling with guilt.

Right after work in the break room, I searched for Hattie. "How's your brother?"

"He's doin' all right. Has a broken wrist, and his arm's in a sling. He was actin' mighty peculiar mumblin' more than he does. I reckon they've given him some medicine. When the doctor tole him he was needed back at the base right quick, his face started a twitchin'. He tried talkin' the doctor into lettin' him stay, which ain't like him to talk to a White person that willfully."

"It's all over the newspapers. It was a terrible explosion. He must've seen some of his buddies die."

Hattie hung her head, speaking to her lap. "Before leavin,' I tole him to come 'round to see me. He didn't answer but started twitchin' agin." She changed the subject. "I got a letter from my Granger. Can y'all read it to me?"

"Sure."

Darling Hattie:

I have plenty of time to write you. I am under arrest in my quarters, as well as over hundred other Negro officers! I'm fine and I don't mean to worry you.

This is what happened. There are two officers' clubs here at the Freeman Field Indiana base. One for the Whites and the other for us, (which we call Uncle Tom's Cabin because it is so rundown). Each day, a small group of our men tried to enter the White officers' club. Last night a small group of us decided to go peacefully into the White officers club. The White Officer of the Day told us only members were allowed. We knew there were White officers in the club who were not members. I went past him to order a beer. The bartender said, "I can't serve you, you're not a member." I asked him, "How can you tell?" He answered, "Because no coloreds belong to the club."

Three of our men were taken into custody and are now in jail. The rest of us are under house arrest. We all knew there was an Army regulation stating the buildings are open to all officers regardless of race and we wanted to test that law.

121

The general told the press that Freeman Field had two clubs; club number one for "trainees," and club number two for use by "instructors only." What he didn't tell the press was there are no Negro instructors! Many of our officers are qualified to be teachers but are never advanced.

We are now charged with insubordination and subject to court martial. We've had to have a quiet strength in order to suffer all the insults. I wish the Whites would recognize that a unified military would only benefit in helping win this endless war.

Sweetheart, try not to fret about me. We continue to fight for the double victory; the war against racism here and the war for our country in the pacific. They have not let us fight overseas yet, but we are a strong group and intend on winning both wars.

You know, Hattie, you look like Lena Horne, but with more substance on you, more lovin' to get my arms around! I was very happy to get your letter and showed all my Army buddies the lipstick kiss you put in at the end of it!

Sorry to hear about your brother Sam.
Keep writing.
Your loving husband, Granger

Hattie took the letter from me, felt it with two fingers, then put it in her lunchbox. She slumped. Her eyes wandered off into the distance. Hopelessness was all over her face. Suddenly, she mumbled, "Arrested..." then rose, got her helmet out of her locker, and left.

Chapter 25: Cuttin' the Rug

On the drive to the dance hall, I unloaded my burden of worry about Sumi and Hattie to Phil. "I got a letter about Sumi, she had the baby."

"How'd that go in a horse stable?" His mouth was pinched with disgust.

"Her husband Hiroshi wrote and said she had to be cut open because her labor went on for two days."

"That's a long time to wait for a baby to come out, isn't it?" He frowned.

"My labors were quick, but two days is way too much stress on a baby. Hiroshi wrote that the nurse only gave her a local anesthetic. He left the makeshift hospital room when they cut her open. When he came back there was a baby, but its heartbeat was faint and might not be normal." I choked on the word *normal*.

Phil patted my leg, his eyes still on the road. "Let's pray for that poor family."

"I have." I smiled a little and continued, "He never said whether she had a boy or girl." My eyes drifted out toward the rain-filled clouds. "Hattie's brother was in the Port Chicago explosion. She said they released him early from the hospital to help clean up the shipyard mess and the bodies of the men killed."

"From what I read in the paper, it must be quite a job." Phil shook his head.

"She's was so upset, and to top it off, her husband was just arrested!"

"What happened? Isn't he a pilot?" Phil's eyes left the road for a quick second.

"He went with some of his buddies to get into a 'Whites only' officers' club."

"That unfortunate girl's been getting an unfair share of bad luck. I always liked what a hard worker she was in class."

Only the car motor could be heard, replacing further conversation with troubled silence.

After reaching the dance hall, we got out and read the sign at the entrance.

Uncle Sam needs your discarded silk and nylon stockings for gunpowder bags.

Please launder and leave here!

I looked down at my ankle socks, missing the silky feel of my stockings on the red kneelers at church.

The slow dances were heavenly as Phil's rough, manly cheek rested on mine. His gentle hand caressed my waist. The dreamy, romantic music of the band pulled us closer and closer together. When they played and sang "As Time Goes By," Phil kissed me.

"A kiss is just a kiss," the words floated up and down my body. It must be our song, I mused, since it followed us everywhere.

The next number, "You Always Hurt the One You

Love" pulled me back to the reality of being a married woman. I stiffened as we danced farther apart.

We did a rousing jitterbug and I counseled myself to enjoy it. I never had danced with Joe. He used to say, "Dancing is something only girls do."

In Phil's cozy automobile, he reached over and held my hand while trying to keep his eyes on the road. "I had a lovely time with you, gal."

I beamed at him as our eyes wandered toward each other's, until he had to look back to the road. Luckily, there weren't many cars around because of the war shortage.

He put his arm around my waist as we waltzed up the front porch steps of my house.

I giggled, "Thanks, I had a wonderful time. You're a snazzy dancer."

I gave him a little peck on his cheek and opened the screen door.

He asked, "Aren't you going to ask me in for coffee?"

Fala wouldn't stop barking his "it's a stranger" bark even though Phil tried every technique to win his affection. I got out a piece of meat from last night's dinner and gave it to Phil so he could get Fala to stop his incessant yapping. Giving up, I swooped up his furry body and put him in the children's room.

I turned from Phil's hungry wanting eyes and put the kettle on. Before I could light the stove, he wrapped his arms around me. My mother's Channel No. 5 and his Allspice aftershave swirled together, drifting us into the bedroom. As our scents fused, twirled, and mingled into one, he whispered in my ear, "You smell delicious!"

We fell onto the bed and Phil placed tiny, delicate kisses up and down my neck. I heard a crinkly noise as he removed a small square white paper envelope from his pocket. After he ripped it open, he waved the cellophane circle proclaiming, "Do not fear; I have a rubber!"

I grabbed him tighter, thinking, This man really cares about me…

Our hands floated on each other's bodies, exploring and craving. His hardness was full of the flow of electricity, like my welder's stinger. We were in slow motion. My entire being shook, spasms of sparks flew about. "Oh, oh, oh…" escaped from my mouth as he entered me.

Chapter 26: Getting Ready

October brought much needed rain, but made getting to and from the Child Development Center more of a chore. My little family all tromped off the bus on our way home. All of us sloshed about the road in our boots.

Billy released my hand, jumped from puddle to puddle, and yelled, "Sploosh!"

I refrained from reprimanding him as Mrs. Ginzberg's high-pitched voice rang in my head, "Let the children be creative. One never knows how this can enhance their future endeavors."

Upon reaching home I retrieved the mail, put it on the kitchen table, and helped the rain-soaked children get into their nightclothes. Edna and Billy fell asleep fast after we had warm soup and toasted cheese sandwiches. I glanced over the bills and saved Joe's letter for last, glad he couldn't spy on my unfaithful activities with Phil.

Dear Lolly:

Good news, I'm getting a leave for Thanksgiving. I received two letters from you today. I want you to write to me every day and put dates on them. This way, I know what order to read them in. One of my buddies here gets a letter from his wife and she numbers them, and for God's sakes would you start using V-mail? Don't you know about it? How are the kids? I miss them sorely. I can't wait to get a home-cooked meal and a warm body to sleep next to — if you know what I mean!

Love, Joe

Hands shaking, I vowed to myself that I would end my love affair with Phil and pretend it never happened. I hoped Joe truly missed me and could be a kinder, more loving person after being gone.

I reread the letter as my temper flared. He is such a know-it-all. I'm not stupid, I know what V-mail is. All my V-mail was used up when I wrote letters for Hattie. I must get around to telling him about my war job...

I chewed at my fingernails.

Chapter 27: A Leave

Thanksgiving came faster than expected. We waited for Joe at the train station. The children were overjoyed watching all the excitement. There were many soldiers who got off the train, and much kissing going on when they reunited with their loved ones.

Joe appeared taller to me and more muscular, if that was possible. He was very dashing in his Navy uniform. After he kissed me, he tapped Billy's diaperless bottom, saying, "Looks like you've lost some weight, sport."

Edna interrupted, "I missed you, Daddy, will you live with us now?"

Instead of answering her, he grabbed me hard and kissed me again. Feelings of security came upon me as I gave him a blissful smile.

On the bus ride home, Joe put his arm around me as each child found a lap. I spent the whole ride thinking what I would say about Fala, wondering if Joe would welcome this new addition to our family.

When we opened the door, Fala rushed toward us, gave only one sharp bark, then rubbed himself on Joe's uniform.

Joe scratched the dog's head. "What's this little mutt doing here?"

Edna spoke right up saying, "That's Fala, and we're babysitting him while Sumi's on vacation."

"Who?" Joe asked.

I spoke fast. "We have a new pet. The children love him. Besides, he's a faithful watch dog for us since you've been away."

Billy went and got his ball and rolled it to Fala, who successfully fetched it every time.

"What a smart dog!" Joe slapped his pant leg, signaling Fala to come. Fala's tongue hung out as he wiggled all over Joe.

"Edna, come help me with the butter," I said with a glowing smile.

She squeezed a capsule of yellow coloring into the oleomargarine. I got out a spoon.

"Now, mash it around to make it yellow."

For our Thanksgiving meal, I had made a make-believe turkey. Turkey meat was too hard to find anyway. I followed a recipe in *Collier's Magazine*. Fashioning meat loaf around four clothespins, I stuck them in a big hunk of hamburger, which made it looked like a turkey. I displayed it proudly on the table.

"The turkey's cute!" Edna flashed her dimples at me.

"Thanks, sweetie, help me fold the napkins."

"That's a turkey?" Joe questioned, then saw my dark expression and lied, "Very clever."

Billy pulled at my skirt. "Can I have pie now?"

"No, that's for dessert. Go find something to play with in your room while your sister helps me set the table."

It's a good thing Joe had me buy all that sugar from the Matsumotos' store, or the pumpkin pie would not have been very sweet.

Joe dragged on his Chesterfield. "I'll teach you how to play cards, son."

I happily hummed "As Time Goes By," placing Mother's good plates and silverware on the special occasion tablecloth.

"Pretty song, Mommy!"

"You've a nice voice too, Edna."

Edna tried singing "Mairzy Doats." It was such a silly song. I helped her along with the words while we put out all the food.

I washed the dishes after our big meal, and Joe surprised me by drying them as the children listened to the "Fibber McGee and Molly Show" on the radio.

After the last dish was put away, he held me close, saying, "I missed you, babe!"

"It's nice being a family again, even if it's for just a few days." I rubbed his rough face, stretched up and kissed him.

"Isn't it bedtime for the kids yet?" Joe raised his eyebrows, then gave me a wink and pinched me on my bottom.

"Ouch!" I startled and laughed. "I'll shut the radio off, then they'll get tired."

I put the children to bed and worried about sleeping with Joe. Would he know that I had been with another man? I dawdled in the children's room until I heard his familiar call.

"Lolly!"

I kissed Billy and Edna goodnight, then slowly headed toward our room.

I turned off the bedroom light.

Joe said, "Keep it on. I want to watch you get undressed."

After I flipped the switch back on, I sat at the end of the bed, shyly took off my dress, and felt as though I was with a stranger.

"Stand up, Lolly, let me have a look at you!"

He was so demanding. It had been a long time since I'd had to take his orders. Inwardly I frowned, but outwardly I forced a smile on my face and pulled off my slip.

"You sure look fit!" He kissed me once, then was inside me in no time.

I couldn't help thinking about Phil's slow lovemaking and surprised myself by releasing a quiet moan.

"Wow, babe, I've never heard you say that before. I guess absence makes the heart grow fonder!"

Yes, I had never made that noise with him before. I guess this was something I learned from being with Phil, and Phil was the one on my mind as Joe came within me.

As my husband snored, I tried to imagine the smell of Phil's aftershave. Joe never wore any and said it was too girlish, nor did he allow me to wear Mother's Channel No. 5, complaining it was too smelly.

The next morning after breakfast, Edna sat at the table with a few crayons and scrap paper while I did the dishes. Joe came in the kitchen for some matches, saw her artwork, and yelled at her.

"What the hell are you drawing, Missy?"

"I've watched all the children making these, they're fun!" Edna eyed her father with wonder.

"Lolly, why's our daughter drawing swastikas, and what other children is she blabbering about?" He dragged hard on his cigarette, exhaling a big puff of smoke.

Before I could answer, Edna proudly told him, "My friends at the day care."

"Fer cryin' out loud, what's she talkin' about?" Joe's temper flared.

"Joe, I had to get a war job, we needed the money. I was going to tell you, but I thought you might get mad."

"Of course I'm mad. Where are you putting our children when you're at this war job? At this day care?" He shook his finger at me.

"Honey," I said, trying to soften the situation, "the children go to the Maritime Child Development Center. It's a very modern place, a school really." I straightened the dusty doily under an old cracked vase.

"What's this so-called war job you got?" His cigarette hung from his mouth as he spoke.

"I'm a welder at the shipyard." My voice quivered. I was confused, not knowing whether to feel proud or guilty.

Joe's eyes bugged out. "Why didn't you tell me? No wonder you hardly ever wrote!" He exhaled smoke all around us. As fast as his bad mood blew in, a good one replaced it. He calmly said, "How much do you make?"

"I make a $1.30 per hour and I've bought a few war bonds even."

"Woooo!" Joe whistled, then added, "How many men do you work around?" His eyes narrowed.

"Some old 4F fellas, but mostly gals. One gal I work with studied to become a ballerina before the war broke out. In the shipyard newsletter it said we have sixty percent of the San Francisco symphony working there!" I spoke fast, trying to gain his reassurance about my job.

Joe ended the subject by abruptly going into his workshop in the garage. As I swept the kitchen floor, I noticed Edna's drawings on the table, snatched them up, and hid the pile on top of the Coldspot. I missed how much quieter our family was without Joe's temper encompassing us.

The next day, we went to Mass as a family, which gave me a warm feeling as we all cuddled in the pew. The children were better behaved than usual, sensing how rare it was for us to be together. The men that were there sat proudly in their uniforms, arms around their wives.

That night in bed after doing my wifely duty, I asked Joe if he wouldn't mind watching the children, since I had to go to work the next day in order to keep my job.

He hesitated, then asked, "How much money did you say they pay you?"

After I told him he agreed to watch Edna and Billy, since it was his last day before shipping out.

I came home after a long day of welding, and cheered right up seeing Joe drawing a ship. He was explaining all the parts on it to Billy. Joe was truly a wonderful father for our children; I swore to myself to never see Phil again. I kissed both of them and sat down to rest my legs, which throbbed from bending all day.

"This gal I work with has a husband in the Tuskegee Air Corps and..."

Before I could finish my sentence, Joe snapped, "Those colored flyers aren't worth a damn!"

I tried to protest, but he turned away from me saying to Billy, "Here on the front of the ship it's called the fore, and the back, aft. Now what's the main body called?"

Billy answered quickly in his squeaky voice, "Hull."

"That's my boy. Someday maybe you'll be a sailor, just like your ol' man!"

Joe's leave was almost over. Seven days seemed way too short. When I saw how well he cared for our children while I worked, it made my marriage to him feel very strong. He almost was like a changed man since joining the Navy. The only time my feelings of love wandered during his stay with us was when he expressed his strong prejudices about other races. We just weren't brought up the same way.

On the last day, Joe packed up his duffel bag and we all took the bus to the train station. The children and I sadly watched the train pull away.

"Mommy, will Daddy come back?"

"Of course, Billy. When the war is over." I bent down and gave him a little hug.

"When will the war be over?" Billy demanded.

"Nobody knows that, stupid!" Edna kicked a pebble as the last train car rolled away in the distance.

I bit my lip, not having the energy to discipline her. We all felt at a loss after Joe left.

Chapter 28: Solitary Confinement

One day at work, Hattie seemed quite distracted during break time. I asked her what was wrong.

With a troubled face she explained, "It's my bruther, Sam. He's locked away in prison now."

"How'd that happen?"

"He went back to work after bein' in the hospital an' wouldn't pick up the bodies of his mates from the explosion. His roommate came by last night tellin' me he's in somethin' called solitary confinement, an' I can't visit him there. He quit cleanin' up after he saw a foot in a boot with no body."

"That's terrible, Hattie. I'm so sorry." I put my arm around her as she sniffled. The back-to-work whistle blew. We got up from the bench and put on our gear.

After work, I got a newspaper to see if I could read any more information about the Port Chicago explosion. Slipping the *Chronicle* with the headline "Port Chicago Mutiny" in my jacket, I saved it for later. A series of breezes bounced off the bay.

That evening I unfolded the newspaper and read:

Port Chicago Mutiny
Fifty Negro men were imprisoned after refusing to do

their job.

*The seamen were taken to the Mare Island Naval Shipyard to load mines and other munitions on the **USS Sangay**, since Port Chicago is presently unable to be used after the explosion.*

Several Seaman disobeyed orders and were taken under guard to a barge used as a temporary military prison.

The new pier at Port Chicago will take one month to reconstruct.

The next day, I waited for Hattie in the break room and ate a sandwich from my lunch bag. "I read the news about the mutiny in last night's paper," I told her when she arrived.

"I sure have my troubles, but it's comfortin' to have a true friend like you to share 'em with." She sat down next to me, not even bothering to open her lunchbox.

"Your brother must've been part of the Port Chicago Mutiny and got charged with refusing to do his duty loading munitions."

"Yesum, Jim came by the room last night, tole me the whole story. Most of the sailors were afraid of loadin' them munitions after the explosion of the ships, 'specially after puttin' body parts in wheelbarrows all day."

Hattie was so forlorn. I tried to cheer her up, but to no avail. She just shut down every time I tried to think up something positive to say, then she left the break room in the middle of one of my sentences. Feeling quite helpless, I had a longing to discuss the mutiny with Phil, but I squeezed my lips together, determined to keep my wedding vows.

Chapter 29: Two Mutinies for Hattie

I read a letter from Diana during my break. Hattie was nowhere to be seen.

Dear Lolly:

It took a while, but my legs have finally recovered, and I am writing this letter while I sit on the wing of a P-40 fighter.

I hope you and your children are doing well. How's your Joe?

Edwin wrote saying he is learning to fly the P-38. It used to be called the "Widow Maker" until these women pilots called the WASPs tested them and showed the men they were safe when flown correctly.

This factory has a charm course I go to on Thursday nights. The instructor teaches us to be feminine and ladylike even though we are filling men's shoes. We learn that factory work does not have to make wives less womanly. This is why most of us use a little rouge for color to liven up our cheeks and reapply our lipstick frequently. In the magazines, Betty Grable encourages us to send our men a pinup photo, like one in a swimsuit, to inspire them to keep on fighting. I have a friend who is coming over on the weekend to take a snapshot of me to "wow" my Edwin. Maybe you should do the same for Joe!

My arms have been killing me because these rivet guns are huge and heavy! I'll never feel helpless around the house again, I am so strong now. When I get home at night I have sore muscles and swollen hands, along with a headache. I try to run a bath just to relax before I go to bed, but most of the time I'm too beat and just fall asleep with my work clothes on. One night, I heard a rivet gun going, the noise of it screeched through my body, then I awoke to find that the gun was really me, squeezing my pillow! I just tell myself it's all for my Edwin.

Whenever anyone complains at the factory, we all say over and over, "Don' cha know there's a war goin' on? Buck up! It's just for the duration!" This one guy always says, "Helping Hitler again?" anytime someone makes a mistake.

One woman had a grinding wheel explode in her face. It left a terrible scar. After she got bandaged up all she said was, "It does hurt, but it's my badge of service for our country!"

I do have oodles of new friends and love to work, I don't mean to complain so much. You must really have a tough time of it, holding down a job and taking care of two small children.

I sure miss you kid,
Love, Sis

My heart ached after reading the letter. It made me wish I could go over my complicated love life with my sister. The thought of writing a letter didn't settle well with me. I knew seeing my troubles in stark black and white was something I wasn't ready to face.

I had not seen Phil in over two months and it was hard on me. I missed our intimate conversations. Sumi was on my mind constantly. I had written her two letters, but had received none in return. I couldn't talk to Hattie about her since she had her own troubles. Every day I brought my lunch in an attempt to avoid Phil, and put an end to my extramarital affair. To gain will power, I would mentally list Joe's favorable attributes. His large, manly body; his boyish dimples; but most of all, he was a good dad and sincerely loved his children.

Hattie came into the break room and cheerfully announced, "I got a letter from my Granger. Will y'all read it for me, Lolly?"

"I'd love to!"

Sweetie Pie...

I stopped a moment. "I adore that he calls you Sweetie Pie!"

Hattie's face brightened as I continued reading:

I'm no longer imprisoned in the barracks in Indiana. We have been flown to Godman Field, Kentucky, because we (101 men) refused to sign a new base regulation that basically reiterates that we can't use the White officers' club. One Negro officer signed and wrote, "This is racial discrimination."

The general put out a notice that said there would be strict segregation of base facilities and all the officers, Negroes and Whites, were ordered to sign this new regulation. The Negro officers refused. We were then arrested and confined to our quarters. The next day, we were transferred under armed guard to Godman Field, Kentucky, where we were placed under house arrest once more.

When we first arrived here, were put in large prison vans that are used to transport German and Italian prisoners of war. Upon getting out, there were 75 military police armed with sub-machine guns. German POWs walked around without guards and seemed to be laughing at us, as if we were the enemy!

We remain under house arrest with no assignments and just play cards all day. We just want to go back to Freeman Field and complete our combat training, then fly our planes overseas to prove that Negroes can help fight this war.

The general said to us, "This country is not ready or willing to accept a colored officer as equal to a White one and we are not in the Army to advance our race. Our primary purpose is to fight for our country to win this war." He ended this speech by adding, "We will not tolerate a mutiny and will weed out any racial agitators!"

I can't help wondering at a time like this, isn't it more important for us to work together so we can successfully fight the war against the nation's enemy overseas?

I sorely miss you, sweetie, and could really use your comfort at a time like this. Please write as soon as possible. Your letters keep me going!

Your loving husband, Granger

"There's that nasty word, 'mutiny.' How can my hubby an' my bruther both be usin' that word?" Hattie said in a high voice as she sadly nodded her head back and forth saying, "Un, un, un."

"In case you didn't know, Hattie, 'mutiny' means rebellion or uprising."

"I figur'd as much."

"It's hard to believe you know two people involved in a mutiny. Hopefully now things will get better for your husband. I think it's necessary that all the Negro officers fight for their freedom. I'm sure they've been feeling pretty useless not being allowed to go overseas into battle. It must've taken guts to put up with those arrogant White officers."

"I suppose you's right, I should count my lucky stars they is both alive."

Hattie took the letter from me. I could tell by her slouching face and shoulders she didn't believe a word I said.

Chapter 30: A Baby and a Thief

Much to my astonishment, a policewoman walked into the break room, followed by Phil.

The officer announced to the entire locker room, "We're here to investigate all the theft reports." She tapped hard on her wooden baton.

Ruby spouted out, "It's about time! Now my brand new welder's jacket is missing and it cost me plenty of spare change. I even put my name on it in red nail polish."

Dottie added, "I had my helmet stolen."

I didn't say a word about my lost lunchbox, as it didn't seem as important as those other items.

The policewoman turned to Phil. "Mr. Cunningham, you do the interviews, I'll check all the lockers.

Phil said in a stern voice, "Mrs. O'Brien, I'll interview you first, meet me outside the door."

I followed him out, and breathlessly said, "I'm not the thief!"

Phil cautiously looked around, then gently caressed my shoulders and melted into my eyes. "Lolly, I've missed you something awful. Where've you been? I volunteered for this job as I figured it would be a great excuse to see you."

"I'm glad you didn't think I would steal anything."

He disregarded that comment, and spoke frantically, "I can't help how I feel about you. When you were in my class I felt your hunger for learning and became physically attracted to you. I know you're married, but I've fallen in love with you. I've never been this close to anyone. I miss our, um, intimacy and our long talks. Please, Lolly, meet me at the canteen again," he pleaded as his finger stroked my cheek, his eyes boring into mine.

My face bunched up. Trying not to cry, I said, "I feel the same way. I'm barely attracted to my husband anymore."

Phil gave me a deep, long kiss.

I pulled away, sniffling. "But he's such a good father."

"All I ask, Lolly, is just be with me until the war's over, then I promise to let you go back to your married life." He pushed his glasses on top of his head as we came back together, nose to nose.

His eyes drew me in once more, and I held his face, gazing into his honey-brown eyes that oozed into mine. I pushed away from him and slipped into the toilet room. I couldn't control my emotions any longer and burst out crying. I washed my face, blew my nose, retied my hair snood and walked back into the hallway. Passing Hattie and Phil, I grinned when I overheard their cheerful conversation. My Joe would never have been caught dead talking to a Negro.

Hattie came back into the locker room with a broad smile and said, "I sure 'nough fancy that man, he's been mighty kind to me."

The policewoman dashed toward Phil. "I've found the stolen items. Come see!"

We all followed. The police officer opened locker 207

145

wider, showing that it was jam-packed full of hard hats, makeup, candy, tools, oranges, all kinds of welding apparel, and my lunchbox. Phil pulled out a jacket and on it in bright red nail polish was the name, "Ruby."

Ruby cursed. "God damn it, there's my new jacket! Where's that thieving Vera? This is her locker!"

Dottie yelled, "That's my helmet!"

The whole crowd of us began to shout, "Vera, Vera, we want Vera!"

Ruby demanded to the policewoman, "Check the toilet!"

The officer squeezed through all of us and banged on the toilet room door. Out came Vera, guilt smeared all over her face. The policewoman didn't say a word, just hand-cuffed her on the spot. All the gals cheered as the "goods" were distributed back to their rightful owners.

The next day, after a sleepless night, I raced through the shipyard searching for Phil. As I made my way through the crowds, I spotted him, waving wildly.

"I knew you'd come, I could feel you missing me!" He held both my hands together warmly.

"I couldn't help it." Holding his hand tightly, I said, "What happened with Vera?"

"She confessed. The officers told me she was fired and locked up. They said she had something peculiar about her, not right in her head. One policewoman told me it's a disease called 'kleptomania.' Vera couldn't help stealing anything she could get her hands on."

"I suspected it was her. She was so strange, never joined in singing or talking to any of us. Once Vera looked me up and down when I was getting dressed. I'm not surprised it was her." My eyebrows rose.

"Tell me, what's new? Have you heard from Sumi?"

I spoke fast, my words tumbled out, happy to share my thoughts with Phil again. "I just got a letter from her."

"Tell me." His eyes intently gazed at me.

"She had the baby, guess I told you that. It was a girl. The baby's doing better and has gained weight. Sumi recovered from the operation, thank God."

The sky was completely cloudless, unusual for winter. A squawky seagull flapped above us.

"I'm glad they're both fine after that gruesome operation." He gently ran his hand over mine, playing with each of my fingers. When his touch came upon my naked wedding band finger, I pulled away.

"I've been on what my mother would call 'pins and needles' worrying about Sumi. The bad part of the letter was the weather. It's nasty here but worse there. She wrote the rains caused the track grounds to be like soggy, sticky black molasses, making it hard to get around without slipping. When it wasn't raining, her family had to deal with horseflies that wouldn't go away. The wind was so cold and piercing it went right through the thin walls of the stable."

"However can she manage with a newborn in that environment?" Phil asked, his face full of compassion.

"Thank goodness her husband's so helpful."

"Go on, did she write any more?"

"She asked if I'd come see her."

"Really? I didn't know visitors were allowed."

"I was surprised, no one under sixteen can go, though."

"I'll watch your children for you."

"That's very kind of you, but I'll take them to the Child Care Center on Saturday and say I have to work. They love it there. On the weekend they get very bored without other kids to play with, anyway." I leaned in and gave Phil a kiss on the cheek, then glanced around, worried that someone had noticed.

"You're lucky to have such a positive friend who can survive in that horrible place. Our government should be ashamed of putting American citizens in camps like that." He spoke with conviction as he drew my body in.

I moved closer to him. "When I read her letters, it makes me anxious, but she has a natural faith to overcome it all. It makes me feel grateful for what I have. I've been knitting a cap at night for her baby."

Phil's eyes held mine. All the noise of the shipyard disappeared. We were in a private world of our own, sharing a sacred closeness.

He broke the silence. "Let's go for a ride Wednesday after work."

"I can't Phil, I promised myself I'd be faithful." I looked up at the sky. A few grey clouds of winter were beginning to form.

"A short drive won't hurt."

"Talking is one thing, but I don't trust myself to be alone with you." My lips formed a pout as my eyes wandered to my tightly folded hands.

The whistle blew. Phil squeezed my shoulder. He said, "I'll pick you up at the canteen after work, bring a picnic dinner."

Before I could protest, he was gone.

Chapter 31: Questions #27 and #28

The ride to the ocean was full of colors. The multi-shades of reds, yellows, and blues filled our eyes as the sun spread the last of its glory throughout the sky for the day. In all this beauty, it was hard to believe there was a war raging on in the Pacific. I had packed extra food in my lunchbox and Phil brought a few bottles of beer. He parked by a small cliff facing the ocean. We sat in silence after we ate, and enjoyed each other's company as we listened to the soothing rhythmic waves.

Breaking the quiet, Phil said, "I haven't had cornbread in a while, it was terrific."

"Thanks. It didn't turn out too bad without real butter. I never can find any. At least it has sugar." Joe's past ranting about hoarding sugar crossed my mind.

"I got a letter from my friend Tom. Remember, I told you about him? He's Japanese-American and worked at the shipyard with me."

"Yes, I remember. You told me he had gotten fired."

Phil wiped his mouth, tucked the napkin back in my lunchbox, and handed me a beer. "In the beginning of the letter it sounded like he was well-adjusted to camp, and he even joined a group that built a lake to beautify the place. It was his idea to make a bridge with islands around it. Here Lolly, have another beer."

"I'm not done with this one. What else did he write?"

"He helped make toy sailboats for the kids to float in the lake."

"Wonder if little Frankie was there?"

Phil shrugged, then continued, "He wrote that on hot days most of the men were angry after they wandered around the racetrack and saw a banner across a hillside outside the camp that read, **ENJOY ACME BEER.**"

I swallowed wrong, causing me to hiccup.

"He's trying to get his parents' books written in Japanese to read, but the guards won't allow it." Phil opened another bottle of beer for himself, then looked over to see if I had finished mine. "A recruiting team came, and they made all the men fill out a questionnaire for a volunteer combat unit."

"They're taking Japanese-Americans into the service now from the camps?" I gasped.

"The questionnaire had 28 questions to determine loyalty and willingness to fight. They forced everyone to fill it out, even his parents and sister!" Phil glanced at my startled face.

"Why did they do that?"

"I don't know. Tom wrote he was upset about two of the questions." Phil pushed another beer at me.

"What were they?" I anxiously drank more beer, even though it was quite bitter.

"Let's see, here it is." He reached into his pocket. "Hummmm," Phil said, running a finger down the letter. "Question 28: Will you swear unqualified allegiance to the United States of America and forswear any form of allegiance or obedience to the Japanese Emperor or any other foreign power or organization?'" Phil held the letter tightly. "His parents didn't want to give up their Japanese citizenship because they weren't born here. If they gave up their allegiance they'd have no country to belong to. I can see their point."

I put my empty bottle on the floor as Phil handed me another.

"This is the other question that Tom didn't like." Phil found the paragraph and read, "Question #27: Are you willing to serve in the Armed Forces of the United States on combat duty, wherever ordered?" Phil looked at me intently and said, "Tom said everyone wanted to answer, 'I'll serve only if the camps are disbanded.' He said that anyone who wrote that or answered no got sent to a prison camp at Tule Lake."

"Those poor people! I wonder how Sumi and Hiroshi filled it out?" I drank another beer and began to feel a bit tipsy.

"Tom wants to join up just to get out of the camp, but is worried about leaving his family." Phil folded up the letter and a scowl formed on his face. "I'm patriotic, but what the government is doing to our people, even if they're of Japanese ancestry, makes me furious! Tom calls it, 'guilt by ethnicity.'" Phil shook the letter at me, adding, "I feel sorry for them and can't wait for this war to be over so they can have normal lives again. Has Hattie heard from her husband?"

"I just read her a letter from him. It said all the Negro officers were released and can finish their training. They hope to help end this war and fly overseas into combat."

"That's a relief he's not under arrest anymore." Phil slugged down another beer.

"Hattie was glad, but everyone did get a permanent conviction in their file that said something like 'displayed a stubborn, uncooperative attitude and lacks appreciation of the high standards of teamwork.'"

"That's lousy!" Phil said.

"I thought so, too. One of their men got convicted of shoving a White officer at the club, was reduced in rank and fined. Wartime has been a strange and difficult time to live in." I reached over, touching Phil's arm in an attempt to soothe his anxiety, as well as my own.

Phil's face brightened. "Let's get out, explore and forget about everybody's troubles. I have a flashlight."

He helped me climb down the steep, narrow cliff as the sun had set and darkness had crept around us. We felt the sand squish beneath our shoes. The beach was ours with no one in sight.

His powerful flashlight shone upon the cliffs, then he pointed it toward a narrow passageway. Phil left my side and leapt joyfully, like a little boy. "A cave! I love caves!" He grabbed my hand gleefully and announced, "Wow, Lolly, our own private cave!"

Phil held me close, and his enthusiastic, warm, passionate kiss turned me to pudding. Feelings overflowed within me. His words 'our own private cave' connected me with his excitement. We trotted through heavier sand, which gave way only a bit since low tide had been with us for a while. He held my hand securely as we swayed and balanced over piles of jagged rocks, the beam of his flashlight guiding us. At last, the light fell upon the rocky passageway. We crouched down like small animals as we both felt the slippery, shiny walls of the hideaway.

My voice echoed as I whispered, "It's warm in here."

The intense salty smell filled my nostrils with delight.

Farther inside the cave it got wider and wider. We could stand, and fell into each other's arms, feeling the thrill as our sensual kisses slowed time. Phil laid his coat on the polished, wave-worn rock floor as we wrapped around each other and became one. We explored each other's bodies, each touch producing a magical sensation.

Satiated from our lovemaking, we listened quietly to delicate water drops falling from the top of the cave. Phil moved the flashlight about and searched all the avenues of the sharp, rippling crannies above us.

Wishes tiptoed all around in my head. I wish we could stay here forever, I wish I wasn't married...

"I wish..." my thoughts within came sweeping out.

Phil quickly put his finger on my mouth, saying, "Hush, let's pretend for now, just this one night."

My thoughts turned to *Casablanca*. I remembered Rick saying, "We said no questions."

Chapter 32: A Telegram

"I got two letters. Can ya'll read 'em for me?" Hattie asked.

"Sure, let me put my jacket away. I'm full of sweat from welding down on the lower deck."

"Read the one from my bruther first." Hattie fiddled with both papers impatiently.

Dear Hattie:

I am having my cellmate write this for me, so you know how I am doing and where I am.

After we cleaned up our mates' bodies and the mess from the Port Chicago explosion, we were transported to another munitions ship on Mare Island. Fifty of us refused to do the work because they would not reassure us that the munitions were not live. As a result, we were locked up and put in the brig.

We also found out many of the White officers were granted thirty-day survivors leave to get away from all of the death. Not one Negro sailor was granted a grievance leave, even though most of us asked for one.

The White officers used to tell us we would be put in the brig if we didn't load the munitions fast enough. Then they would race us, betting which division could load the fastest. When their superiors came by they told us to slow down. Now you know why the explosion most likely happened. We all firmly believed the munitions <u>did</u> have live fuses, unlike what we were told.

Admiral Wright said to all of us that although loading ammunitions was risky, if we didn't do our jobs that death by firing squad was a greater hazard. This is probably why the rest of our men are still loading munitions, but are still not trained on how to do this dangerous job.

I don't know what is going to become of us; we are awaiting trial. I'd rather be here in this prison barge, at least I have a chance of staying alive.

I have been having many nightmares, when the lights go out, like memories of the sound of the blast and of my friends dying, waking me up full of sweat.

Please find someone to help you write back to me. Your letters keep me calm.

Your Brother,
Sam

"Oh my God, Hattie, those stupid officers were racing the sailors? No wonder there was an explosion!"

"Sweet Jesus, my poor bruther! Un, un, un. What would Mama say?" Hattie shook her head so hard her snood almost fell off. "I can't say I blame 'um for quitin'. Like he says, at least he's alive."

"I've read all the newspaper reports and the whole explosion is a terrible tragedy. You should feel lucky he survived it."

"Yes'um, I'm sure you is right." Hattie held her face in her hands. A few minutes went by as she reached into her coveralls and pulled out a second letter. "Maybe this'll be more better."

I studied what she was holding and gasped. "Hattie, that's not a letter; it's a telegram!"

"Woe is me, more trouble."

I grabbed it from her and read fast:

Western Union Telegram: I regret to inform you, your husband, Lieutenant Granger D. Calhoun, has been missing in action since 4 August. If further details or other information of his status are received, you will be promptly notified.
The Adjutant General

Hattie took the telegram from me, put her lunchbox in her locker, and slouched out without a word.

157

Chapter 33: The Racetrack

After I kissed the children goodbye at the Center, I headed to the bus on MacDonald to get to San Bruno. Standing in my welder's uniform, I watched the busy street. The town was bursting with people. I could hardly recognize it. There were many colors of folks with an assortment of languages that filled the air. It was nice to get away from the city for the day. I knitted on the bus and finished the pink cap for Sumi's baby just before getting off.

Watching out the window, I saw a long line of people in front of a cold, metal, barbed wire fence and figured this was probably the place. Sure enough, the bus driver bellowed out, "Tanforan."

It's good Sumi told me to arrive earlier than 10 A.M., I thought.

I hoped the line to get in was not too long, since visiting was permitted for only two hours.

Streams of motorists on the street rolled down their windows and gaped at the Japanese-Americans behind the fence. Several yelled, "Look at the Japs!"

After the official inspection and embarrassing search, I was pointed toward the grandstand. I was quite shaken up as I passed the guard towers, watching men pacing with rifles on their shoulders. I saw row upon row of horse stables. No wonder Sumi wrote that she got lost all the time. In front of the stalls, lines of laundry blew in the light breeze of December. Beautiful, well-tended victory gardens were planted between the "barracks." I noticed hand-lettered signs on some of the stable doors, several humorously read, *Inner Sanctum, Stall Inn,* and even *Sea Biscuit.* Sea Biscuit had actually raced there, which brought to mind the harsh reality that the horse stables were now homes at a racetrack.

I climbed high into the bleachers, and entered a large room filled with the commotion of hugging, crying, package opening, and card playing. Many of the Japanese-Americans were knitting — young, old, female and male! One man in the corner was trying to play a flute above all the noise. A lively craps game was in progress.

Sumi and I found each other and embraced with the baby between us. I wiped the tears from my eyes.

Sumi raised her voice above the crowd. "I missed you so much!"

Holding in my misery after walking through the camp, my words caught. "I did too. Your baby's beautiful! I knitted her a cap." I placed it on her small head, but she quickly took it off. This made Sumi and me laugh as we relaxed, able to renew our friendship once again.

"Let's talk outside, that way we can hear each other." Sumi put the baby's cap back on. "This grandstand room is wonderful. We've had talent shows, pageants, and dances in here. It really boosts everyone's morale." Sumi shifted the baby onto her other hip as the baby babbled, "DDDDDDD."

I smiled and put my finger into her tiny hand. She grasped it tightly, shaking it.

Sumi straightened out the cap. "Thanks for the hat. It's very nice of you. How did you find the time to come all the way here after working at the shipyard?"

"It's an exhausting job, but the Child Development

Center provides meals to bring home after work, so I don't have to cook." I patted the baby's head and felt satisfied the cap fit so well and made her look so cute.

"That's clever of them to provide that service."

"The food's not too bad, either. Can I hold the baby? You never told me her name."

Sumi passed the skinny little thing from her hip into my arms. "This is Eleanor."

"Cute name," I lied and cuddled the baby. The Roosevelts didn't deserve Sumi's patriotic gesture of using their names. "Where's Frankie?"

"At the new school, it's over there." Sumi pointed at a building, but they all appeared the same to me.

I gazed out beyond the camp at the gorgeous panoramic view of the rolling hills of San Bruno and noticed the beer sign that Phil had told me about.

"Frankie's new teacher used to teach in Berkeley, Miss Wakatsuki. Thank the good Lord our children get good care and training here. Frankie goes to school every day, so I have time alone with the baby."

I playfully sailed Eleanor through the air as she giggled a delicious baby laugh. "I've forgotten how sweet six-month-olds are."

Eleanor grabbed my loose hair and tried to put it in her mouth saying, "MMMMMMM."

I laughed, adjusting the cap on her head as she grabbed it off and tossed it on the ground once again. "You silly little girl," I said, cuddling her tighter.

There was construction going on everywhere. Carpenters made loud hammering noises below us.

Sumi pointed. "Over there's one of the mess halls. It's hard to teach Frankie any manners; everyone hurries through their meal, guzzling it down. The children run and play around the dining hall instead of eating. That way is one of the public bathhouses. They're awful; the flush toilets are always broken. Only half-partitions separate them. Some of us pinned up newspapers and set up boards in front for privacy. The showers are either too hot or too cold. The Army put chlorine foot basins in front of all the shower rooms for sanitation. Most of us avoid the nasty things."

"It sounds very primitive. I'm so sorry you have to stay here." I reached out to touch her arm.

Sumi ignored my comment and continued, "The older women from Japan don't like the showers and found a wooden tub to bathe in. The building with the flag by it, that's the post office." She waved her hand. "It's a busy place because all packages have to be inspected. Over there is a church and two more that way."

"I'm glad you have churches," I said glumly.

"It's comforting to go to the services." Sumi touched my shoulder to reassure me.

I managed to produce a little smile.

"The canteen's in the middle, but there's usually nothing to buy. When there are things for sale everyone shows up and it's too crowded. Of course, living here is all about lines. We have to line up for everything. Most of the time we order things we need from the wish catalog."

"What's that?"

"Montgomery Ward or Sears and Roebuck books."

"How do you get money?"

161

"At first we didn't receive any for working, then we got $8-$16 per month for full-time work, depending on the job." Sumi continued, "Over there's the Assembly Center where we elected our own people to an Advisory Council. Last week the Army ordered that only American citizens could be elected."

My mouth hung open as Sumi explained life in Tanforan. I could scarcely stomach hearing any more, but she was yearning to tell me everything.

"I hate when the Caucasian camp police walk their beats, searching for contraband, looking for anything suspicious. Now we have our own people as house captains who make the rounds to take enrollment twice a day. Over there are the laundry buildings, where we can wash, dry, and iron our clothes. It's continually out of hot water and the boiler's blown up several times. Hiroshi and I trade off doing the wash after midnight, then we get a washtub and are guaranteed hot water."

"You have a wonderful husband. Where is he?" I tried to be upbeat and change the subject.

"He's off playing Goh or Shogi."

Sumi saw my questioning face.

"That's chess and checkers. It keeps his mind off thinking about the store." Sumi gave Eleanor a cracker, and hesitantly asked, "Lolly, I need a favor. I know you don't have much time."

"I'm glad to do anything for you," I said eagerly.

"I was hoping you could walk by our store and see if the Soleskys are keeping a watch on it."

"I could on my day off. I'll write and let you know how it is."

"Thanks, it would help Hiroshi's worrying and mine. Would you like to see where we live?"

I politely said, "OK."

On the walk to her barracks, the stench of stagnant sewage filled the air. We went by row after row of horse stalls as Sumi read the numbers to find her way.

I tried to keep the conversation cheerful by saying, "The gardens are beautiful. It looks like they get great care and attention."

"Thanks, they do. Many of our people used to be truck gardeners and nurserymen."

We came to row number 207, "Apartment" 58. It was semi-dark inside with only one window. A swinging half dutch door divided the stall into two rooms. I noticed it was worn down by horses' teeth marks. Up above was open space that extended the full length of the stable. I heard snores, babies crying, people arguing, and even jitterbug music. The crevices and large knotholes in the walls didn't make for much privacy.

There were three spring-type Army cots with hand stuffed mattresses full of straw. The beds hugged a wall that had dead insects buried within the slap-dash whitewash job. On a wooden apple box was a hot plate plugged onto the side of a single electric light bulb socket that dangled from the ceiling in the middle of the animal stall.

Sumi watched me examining the grass between the planks of the floor as I reflected back on the ink drawing she had mailed me.

"The first month was the hardest. Now at least the walls have been whitewashed. We were told we'd be getting linoleum soon to cover the grass. Most of us tried throwing

163

lye down to get rid of the manure and urine smell."

A mouse suddenly scampered over my shoe. I let out a little squeal as Sumi went after it with a broom. Hand-sewn print curtains covered the windows and the same fabric was on the makeshift shelves.

"Lovely curtains," I said, and felt the flowered fabric.

Sumi proudly smiled, "I sew when Eleanor's napping."

The manure smell was pervasive; I distracted myself from it by viewing all of Sumi's hand-painted pictures tacked up on the walls. It was like viewing a story of her internment. The first drawing showed Sumi and Hiroshi packing. In the next one, they were with other families, and all were carrying suitcases and wearing baggage labels with family numbers. One of the first paintings of the stall showed dirt on the floor with bugs and spider webs in the corners. Her last picture was precious, showing Frankie playing with other children in a clean, new classroom.

"Sumi, I can't believe how talented you are. I hope when you get out of here that you'll be able to paint beautiful scenic paintings and sell them." I looked at all of them wistfully, and reached into my blouse to hold my cross, then remembered I had removed it after the safety meeting long ago.

"That's sweet of you to say. I take classes here with a former professor of art from U.C. Berkeley, Chiura Obata. There are six hundred students, all ages, and ninety art classes to choose from. I'm beginning to perfect my paintings. It gives me a sense of calmness and harmony. You know, I'm named for a Japanese painting method called 'Sumi.'"

"Really? What's that?" I asked.

"It's a technique of wash painting. A black ink stick made from burnt pinewood soot is ground over an ink stone to get the ink, then water is added. A bamboo brush is used to paint with."

"Sounds fascinating!" I exclaimed, admiring the paintings once again. I looked into her beautiful dark eyes and asked, "Tell me, Sumi, I've been worried. How are you really holding up?"

"I'm doing better than when we first got here and I was pregnant. I'm enjoying my new baby girl." Sumi touched Eleanor's cheek with her finger as the baby babbled delightfully. "There are improvements made every day and I'm getting used to it."

I glanced around the confined stall and found it hard to believe her, but hoped it was true. "I miss visiting you with my kids at your store." My watery eyes turned downward toward the grassy cracks.

"I'm grateful to have a friend like you from the outside." Sumi's eyes were also tearing as she put her arm around my waist. We strolled toward the exit of the camp. "How's Fala? We miss him."

"He misses you, but is happy to be with Billy and Edna. He's been waiting patiently to go back to his real home." I reached out and hugged my friend tightly, trying to keep in a flood of tears about to escape.

Sumi returned my affection, then stoically moved away mumbling, "I will see you soon."

Sadness draped over me as I held in my emotions. The ride home was long, lonely, and depressing. The scenery out of the bus window became a monotonous blur as Sumi's life at the Tanforan Racetrack darted about in my mind.

Chapter 34: A Barber Shop

I pushed the cart with my two children in tow. The walk brought back a whole assortment of mixed memories. I had been going to a store in the opposite direction of the Matsumotos' since their internment; that way the children wouldn't ask me questions about Sumi's family.

"I brought my jacks to play with Frankie!" Billy skipped behind Edna and me.

"We aren't going to that store, stupid," Edna said with a know-it-all look on her face that matched her father's.

"Don't say that, Edna, it isn't very lady-like. Billy, I'm sorry; we're just checking on the Matsumotos' store. They're not there right now."

"Where are they? I want to see Frankie!"

I gathered up my patience. "They're in a different place, but they'll be back soon."

"Why did they move?" Edna yanked my skirt.

"Look, there's the store and the American flag." I rushed ahead.

Edna caught up to me. "Look at that pretty striped pole the Matsumotos put up."

My mouth opened in surprise as I saw a new sign on the store window:

EARL RAY'S BARBER SHOP

"Let's go to Solesky's, maybe they have ice cream." I walked rapidly down the block.

"I want the chocolate kind," Billy sang out behind me.

"I don't want any, it always tastes like the chalk at school," Edna whined.

We rounded the corner. I was glad to distract the children away from the Matsumotos' store. We walked into Solesky's. I took a patient breath and politely said to the owner, "Hello, Mr. Solesky. How are you today?"

"Fine, thank you. What can I get for you?"

"Is there any ice cream available?"

"Just ice pops."

"I'll take two, and the *Chronicle*."

With the children busy licking their sweets, I leaned toward Mr. Solesky and angrily whispered, "What happened to the Matsumotos' store?"

Mr. Solesky snapped, "Can't you see, lady? It's a barber shop now."

"Weren't you supposed to watch it until they got back?" My eyes narrowed.

He laughed. "You think they're coming back? It makes more money as a barber shop than a vacant store, anyway." He got out a broom, sweeping it away from us.

I grabbed Edna and Billy, placing their little hands on the cart. On our way out of the store, smarty-pants Edna said quite loudly, "Mama, weren't you going to get other groceries?"

167

"Not today, we need to get home." I moved the cart way too fast as the children tried to keep up with me.

My heartbeat slowed down halfway home as I sang, "Swingin' on a Star," ending further discussion from the children about the Matsumotos.

Would you like to swing on a star?

Carry moonbeams home in a jar?

And be better off than you are,

Or would you rather be a mule?

Edna's beautiful little voice carried the refrain, *"Would you like to swing on a star,"* with perfect clarity.

Billy giggled when he heard me singing, *"A pig is an animal with dirt on his face. His shoes are a terrible disgrace. He has no manners when he eats his food. He's fat and lazy and extremely rude!"*

We had a ball and added our own animals to the lyrics. Edna cleverly added Fala to the song. Billy learned the refrain by the time we reached home. Once in the quiet house, the barbershop stripes went around and around in my mind like a tornado building up momentum.

Chapter 35: Topaz: The Jewel of the Desert

After intimacy in our secretive, wondrous cave, I went back to meeting Phil once a week at the canteen. We continued to share news about the private war that raged here in our own country.

"Have you heard from Sumi?" Phil's voice was full of warmth and concern.

Even though we hadn't met each other's friends, as time went by we shared them with a familiar closeness.

"Her family's relocated to an established camp." I got out some food from last night's dinner and took a bite.

"Where have they put them now?" Phil asked, clicking his tongue.

"They're in Topaz, Utah."

"What did she say that was like? I hear there are 16 makeshift Japanese detention camps now, all in remote states away from the coast. I'm waiting to hear from Tom to see whether he has moved."

"She said everyone had smiles on their faces, happy to leave the racetrack. On the last days at Tanforan, they held a Mardi Gras with a parade. The way she described the train ride to Utah sounded like a nightmare." I looked away from Phil, trying to find the energy to tell him about it.

"Why, what happened?"

"She wrote the train ride with two kids was difficult because all the shades were kept down so people from the outside couldn't look in. Plus the gas lights didn't work well and at one stop someone threw a brick in a window even though there were armed guards at each exit." I tried to eat my lunch to avoid Phil's face and continued, "She said the trip took three days. Lots of children got sick, including hers, from the over-heated old train."

"I wonder how the food was?"

"She wrote it was good, but hard to enjoy because of all the crying going on."

"I hope for her sake the new camp will be better than the old one." He gave me a cookie, trying to ease my anxiety.

I shook my head and refused the dessert. "Me, too." I released my balled up fist. "I have bad news about Hattie."

"What now?" Phil raised his voice above the canteen chatter.

"She got a telegram. Her husband's missing in action. She's quite shaken up about it and wouldn't talk to me." My hands clenched up again.

Phil met my eyes. "Don't worry, sweets, they'll find him. There's the whistle, let's go to the ship launching together. It'll keep our mind off our problems."

⚓   ⚓   ⚓

There must have been over 5,000 people on the deck of the *SS Red Oak*. I proudly stood with my hand over my heart, saying the Pledge of Allegiance with everyone. An immense American flag waved in the bay breeze. It was a glorious occasion; the ship was finished and ready for the final launching. I scanned the deck.

You'd think you were at a meeting of the Allied Nations, I thought as I surveyed this. Chinese, Poles, Czechoslovakians, French, Norwegians, Scottish, Irish, English, and Italians, all of them American citizens. A gust of wind streaked across the bay, blowing many of the workers' caps off.

After the pledge, a clergyman said a prayer of blessing. Then the Hollywood stars followed. Dinah Shore and Lena Horne, holding bouquets of red roses, congratulated us on a job well done. Mr. Bing Crosby himself gave a lovely speech filled with praise, and ended it by saying, "A new ship is about to be born; our men will bring it to life and we will win this war!"

Dinah broke a bottle of champagne on the bow as everyone cheered. Flash after flash from cameras went off from the press. It was a proud day of honor and achievement, causing huge smiles on everyone's face. I buttoned my top button from the sharp wind, and thought about tomorrow with another new ship to build. Building the *SS Red Oak* had only took a few months. Each ship after took less and less time.

Phil affectionately pulled a piece of confetti from my hair. "What shipyard will you be in now?"

"Yard two, I'll be working on The *SS Robert E. Peary*."

"The *Peary!* I heard it will be used as a publicity stunt to win the record in building a Liberty Ship in the shortest amount of time. There was a Kaiser ship in Oregon that only took ten days. The *Peary* will try to beat this record. You may find yourself working a lot of overtime."

"I'll do the best I can. Don't you know there's a war goin' on?" I said with a wink and chuckle.

Phil laughed. "The first Liberty Ship was the *SS*

171

Patrick Henry. It took 70 days to build it in '41. I worked on that one. Most ships now take 60 days. Hey, since you're off early, let's go to lunch in town before you pick up your kids."

At the diner, Phil read me a letter he received from his friend Tom.

Dear Phil:

We have all been relocated from Tanforan. We were tagged like luggage once again and sent to an isolated, dry and dusty place called Topaz, Utah. On the long trip there, I could see nothing but bleak landscape, which included miles and miles of alfalfa. A rumor circulated during the train ride that we would all be bombed to death when we got to Topaz. This rumor dissipated upon arrival when we were pleasantly surprised to hear a band of former Boy Scouts from Berkeley, who welcomed us with songs. Then I noticed the barbed wire, the guards in towers, hundreds of low black tar-papered military-style barracks and I knew once again we were virtual prisoners in our own country! We were placed in holding pens, like a human zoo.

Everyone has dusty, flour barrel appearances because Topaz is a cold desert that blows alkaline dust particles all over the place, including the cracks in the unfinished barracks. We even wear scarves inside to keep the dust out of our faces.

To think that Topaz, Utah, is called "A Jewel in the Desert." What a laugh!

Please write. It's nice to have letters from the "outside."
Your friend, Tom

"Gosh Phil, it's so depressing. When will this war ever end?"

Phil reached across the table and patted my hand.

172

"We defeated the Germans in Stalingrad, but then they sank twenty-seven of our merchant ships in the Atlantic. You're right, the end of the war doesn't appear to be in sight. Have you heard from Sumi?"

"No, but I must confess, I'm glad."

"Why?"

"After visiting her at Tanforan, she asked me to check up on her store and I think it was sold behind her back!"

"What makes you say that?"

"I went there with my kids and it was a barber shop."

"How the hell can that be legal?" Phil stirred his spoon harder in his coffee.

"Even if I do hear from Sumi, I won't tell her. She has enough to worry about."

That night I listened to the news broadcast:

"Dillon Myer, National Director of the War Relocation Authority, stated to the press today, 'There are approximately 40,000 young people below the age of twenty years old in the Japanese relocation centers. It is not the American way to have children growing up behind barbed wire and under the scrutiny of armed guards.'"

"Then why do they continue to build more internment camps?" I murmured, slipping into a dark mood.

Chapter 36: Port Chicago Mutiny

I ran into Hattie on the *SS Peary*. She was not her usual chipper self. Our short conversations made me think she was probably worrying about her missing husband and brother in prison.

Clamping on the ground cable from a Lincoln generator, we dragged the cables around all day. We leaned and kneeled, trying to keep up the pace to help make the record for shipbuilding. I wove my stinger back and forth, making rows and rows of shiny dots, glad I was getting quite proficient at welding. Confidently, I thought, I can burn rod with best of them and lay a damn good bead!

During break time Hattie said, "I'm glad we is still workin' together. I got a letter from Sam. Can you read it for me?"

"Sure, but have you heard from your husband?"

Her downcast face gave me the answer as she slowly said, "No," then handed me the letter from Sam.

Dear Hattie:

Fifty of us went to court where we were charged with mutiny. Our sentence: we are now reduced in rank to seaman apprentice, 15 years hard labor followed by dishonorable discharge. I am now in the Federal Correctional Institution on Terminal Island in San Pedro Bay. I did the best I could to serve my country, but look at where I ended up. I hope you can find someone to help you write to me because you are my only connection with the outside world.

Your Brother, Sam

Hattie's down-turned face and tight lips made me feel so distraught. I waited a few moments. "I'll write a letter for you."

She rose quietly from the bench saying, "Thank ya, maybe tomorra."

I saw tears roll down her face before she left the break room.

When we finally welded the last pieces of the ship together, a roar of cheers rang throughout. Our foreman announced, "We broke the record. We built the *Peary* in four days!"

The following month, after I got the children to sleep, I went through the newspaper to find any news about Port Chicago. It wasn't in the headlines, but I found it buried toward the end.

Port Chicago Mutiny: Negro Sailors Face Trial

On July 17, in Port Chicago, Contra Costa County on the Southern banks of Suisun Bay, two ships, the SS O'Brien *and* SS Quinault *were blown up after munitions were loaded. This explosion has been the worst home front disaster since the war began.*

The surviving sailors were relocated to Mare Island to continue their work. Fifty Negro seamen refused and were put in the brig. The sailors pleaded not guilty. The trial, known as the Port Chicago Mutiny, lasted for over five weeks.

During the trial several facts were exposed. The powered winches for loading had signs of wear and many hasty repairs were made to them. There was a training building for the stevedores to learn how to load munitions properly and it was never used. The munitions were packed extremely tight and were difficult to pull out of the rail cars. Some of the sailors reported many of the naval shells were damaged and leaked dye from their ballistic caps before the explosion. The seamen were told that the munitions were not active and could not explode because they would be later armed with fuses upon arrival at the combat theater. Only Negro sailors loaded munitions and they were forced to compete for speed by betting White officers.

The National Association for the Advancement of Colored People revealed the issue that the Negro sailors were never allowed to raise in rank. They also wanted to know why the White officers were granted survivors' leave and the Negro sailors were not. The defense attorney stated that the sailors should have been granted survivors' leave, because they were all in a state of shock from the horrific explosion and the subsequent cleanup of human body parts belonging to their former battalion mates.

The final verdict stated that 208 Negro sailors were to be convicted of disobeying orders, with each to forfeit three months' pay.

Fifty of the defendants were found guilty of mutiny and charged with deliberate purpose and intent to override superior military authority. They were reduced in rank to Seaman Apprentice and sentenced to 15 years of hard labor to be followed by dishonorable discharge.

My eyes were bleary, fatigued from overtime. The final news about the Port Chicago Mutiny depressed me. I put down the newspaper and snapped on the radio.

"A record-breaking Liberty Ship was built, the SS Robert E. Peary, *named after an American Arctic explorer.*

The ship was assembled in four days, 15 hours, and 29 minutes at the Kaiser Shipyards in Richmond. There were 250,000 parts weighing over 14,000,000 pounds. At one minute past midnight the 200-ton keel was lowered into place. This feat was accomplished because the keel was previously assembled and prefabricated in a factory, then moved to Richmond by railroad flat cars.

Yard number two won the competition for speed in this truly amazing publicity stunt. After the final fitting out, she will go to war in ten days and carry 17 U.S. Naval Armed Guards with 43 Merchant Mariners.

Most Liberty Ships take two months to build and are presently being built in thirteen states by 15 companies in 18 shipyards.

Congratulations Ship Yard Two!"

All the facts about the ship I had just finished building exhausted me and I fell asleep on the couch, never making it to the bedroom. "On to the next ship!" I shouted out in a dream.

Chapter 37: An Army of Minorities

When I met Phil at the canteen the next day, I told him all about the Port Chicago Mutiny.

Phil shook his fist. "I hate to say it, but between the Negroes and the Japanese-Americans, we're damned lucky to be white. They have their own wars to fight right here on the home front! That reminds me, I got a letter from Tom. He joined up."

"They're really letting Japanese-Americans fight in the war?"

Phil nodded. "They changed their status and aren't classified as 4C, 'enemy alien.' The way this war is dragging on, the government is desperate for more soldiers."

"Does this mean the internment will end for them?"

"I'm afraid not."

"When Tom's on leave he has to go back to the camp?"

"It's hard to believe, but I guess so. I'll read you his letter, it's a long one." Phil sadly reached into his shirt pocket and slowly pulled it out like it was a piece of heavy metal from the shipyard.

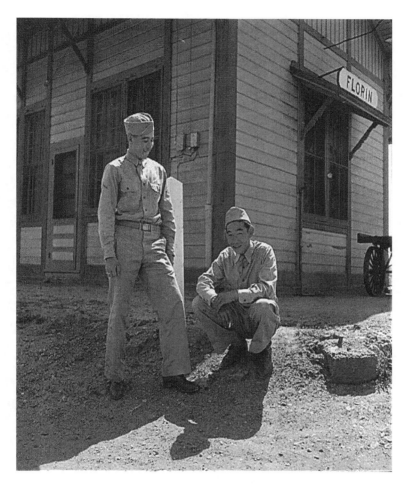

Japanese-American Army soldiers

Dear Phil:

After a group of us petitioned the government to allow us to join the Army, I signed up too. The Army wanted 1,500 volunteer Nisei (Japanese born here) and over 10,000 responded! We are no longer classified as 4C, enemy aliens. Many of us volunteered with the hope that maybe they'll release our families earlier if we show our trustworthiness and are a valuable asset to this war.

Joining up was the only way I could prove my loyalty to the U.S. My sister Mori joined the Women's Auxiliary Army Corps, now at least I don't have to worry about her. I am concerned about leaving my parents, but the internment community in Topaz will take good care of them.

I am now in the 442nd Army Battalion stationed in Mississippi. Our motto is "Go For Broke!"

The 442nd joined together with the 100th Battalion, their motto is: "Remember Pearl Harbor!" They are made up of Hawaiians and we have had a terrible time getting along with them. Their faces may look like ours, but they sure don't sound like us with their carefree kind of language and dress. When they are not in uniform they wear loud, wild shirts and girl-type necklaces called "leis." The Hawaiians go barefoot all the time and are not used to wearing boots. They call us mainlanders "stuck-up" and we call them "buddaheads." This is from the Japanese word "buta," meaning "pig." They in turn call us "kotonks," after the sound of an empty coconut falling on the ground or like a head hitting a wall during a fist-fight.

The hostilities between our two groups slowly heightened. The White officers questioned us that if we continued to have so much friction during basic training in Mississippi, then how were we going to get along overseas in battle? To solve this mounting problem, we were all brought on a trip to Jerome, a nearby internment camp in Arkansas. The 442nd (mainlanders) stayed on different sides of the buses than the 100th (Hawaiians.) The Hawaiians had a gay ol' time playing their guitars and ukuleles (these are small guitars). As soon as they saw the barbed wired fences with White Army men pointing machine guns at all the interned Japanese families, they got real quiet. Come to find out, in Hawaii only a selective, suspicious group of Japanese people were interned. Nowhere near the amount of our people on the mainland. They were going to send all the people of Japanese descent to a nearby island called Molokai, but it never happened. They would have lost one third of the entire population of Hawaii if they had. Besides, they needed a labor force to rebuild Pearl Harbor after the bombing.

The Hawaiians felt so humble when they saw that the families had set aside one week's ration of food to throw a party for all of us.

On the way back to the barracks in Mississippi, there was a calm discussion about what our internment camps were like and not once did they play any loud music. We all get along well now after they realized the heartbreak our battalion has gone through.

We have been well trained now, but are still not being sent overseas. I don't feel we can really prove our loyalty until we are.

I enjoy your letters about the home front. Keep writing,
Your friend, Tom

"I'm shocked that they're taking Japanese-Americans out of the camps and training them to be soldiers without ending the internment. I hope Hiroshi doesn't join up and leave Sumi all alone. The letter I just got from her didn't mention him, but she wrote about a terrible incident at Topaz."

"What's that?" Phil asked as he gave my arm a comforting pat.

181

"An elderly man she was friends with was shot to death at the camp."

"My God! How did that happen? I thought the camps were peaceful places."

"She wrote the MP on duty said he was too close to the fence, was warned many times to move, didn't, then the guard shot him. It turns out he was hard of hearing."

"From what I hear about Topaz, even if someone did escape, where the heck could they go in the middle of a desert, anyway?" Phil demanded.

"How true! Sumi said after the funeral a block meeting was held and that's what other people thought."

We both sat in silence, brooding over that piece of dismal news.

Chapter 38: Red Tail Pursuits

From the 125-amp Lincoln generator, I clamped the ground cable to a sheet of metal, took the stinger, and selected the right number rod from the box. My arms hurt from dragging the cables around, and my knees swelled from all the kneeling and leaning.

Hattie rushed in, waving a letter. "Lolly, Lolly I do believe this is a real letter from my Granger!"

"Thank the Lord," I said, snatched it from her, then read it out loud.

Sweetie Pie:

I am alive! The Army told me they sent you a telegram saying I was missing.

I was on a mission flying my pursuit escorting a White bomber crew, when my plane was shot down over Belgrade (this is a city in a Southeastern European country called Serbia).

The enemy gunned me down in my red-tail P-51 Mustang. I was able to parachute out of my disabled plane and landed in a garden. Shortly thereafter, a teenager with a pistol came up to me and said, "Hello." (It turns out it was the only English word he knew!) The look he gave me told me he had never seen a Negro before, but when he bent over, felt the insignia on my uniform and then smiled, I could tell he knew we were allies.

The young Serb found a hiding place for me in a two-wheel cart under some straw. His family moved me from one Serb's barn to another and safely hid me for 39 days from the Nazis! These foreign people were very kind to me. One family even took me to a barbershop to get my overgrown hair cut. (This surely would've never happened in our hometown in Alabama!)

Thirty days later, I was joined with eleven other downed Americans and we went right back to flying missions.

We are a very proud group. All the White pilots ask for us because we haven't lost a bomber yet! Our all-Negro 332nd Fighter Squadron painted over 72 Pursuits with very bright, insignia red paint. This way the all-White bomber crews can follow us as we escort them to safety and protect them from the enemy. They know we would give our lives for our country. We continue to fight for the "Double V": victory over Hitler overseas and victory over racism in America.

Honey babe of mine, I can't begin to tell you how sorely I miss and need you. Please keep me in your prayers, as I know you will.

Your Lovin' Husband,
Granger

Hattie's face puffed up and her eyes became liquid. I felt her burden dissipating as I held her in my arms. She let loose, her body shaking. I could barely keep from crying myself and thought, She deserves this good news after finding out her brother is to remain in prison...

Tuskegee Airman

Chapter 39: The Lost Texans

It was January, a new year with a fresh start. Maybe this would be the year the war would end. That night I lay in bed with two letters to read. I remained in my work clothes, stretched out, and turned on the lamp. First, I listened to the radio.

"The Japanese-American interment has now ended. On this day, January 2nd, 1945, the exclusion order has been rescinded.

The Supreme Court ruled this past December that detainment of loyal citizens is unconstitutional.

They are free to go back to their former homes after 2 1/2 years and have been given $25.00 with a train ticket."

"Hooray!" I said out loud, then became sad again after I read Sumi's tragic letter. I wasn't looking forward to telling Phil about it. The next day, I found Phil and joyfully told him the news about the internment ending. Being the intelligent man he was, he knew all about it.

"At least the war on the home front is over. Here's a letter from Tom." Phil handed it to me as we sampled the new "Wendy the Welder's" lunch special of the day.

Dear Phil:

I am glad to receive your letters. It gives me a sense of hope to hear about the normal world of welding that does not include information about internment camps or war.

Our 442ⁿᵈ regiment (Nisei mainlanders) joined the 100ᵗʰ regiment (Hawaiians) in Belvedere, Northern Italy. We surrounded the Germans and in one afternoon got them to surrender. For that bravery, we were awarded the highest honor, a Presidential citation.

The next feat was to liberate the town of Breyere from the Germans. With only one day of rest, we received orders to rescue the 141ˢᵗ, known as "the lost battalion of Texans." The Germans had them surrounded, no other Army troop had been successful in liberating the Texans yet. The Texans had no food or water for seven days. They were quite shocked to see us short people, who looked like the enemy, rescue them from the Nazis!

When thinking back on it, the Army considered us expendable, because we did successfully rescue the 211 Texans, but we lost 216 of our people with 856 wounded! The only consolation being that if we succeeded in the mission we knew no one would ever doubt our loyalty.

The general had us all assemble to receive an award when he demanded, "I want _all_ the men here." Our commanding officer said, "General what you see _are_ the only men left!"

The Army now calls us the "Christmas Tree Regiment," because we received so many decorations. We continue to set out trying to break every Army record there is.

Thanks for all your support, Phil. Your correspondence has really kept me going.

Your Friend, Tom

"The patriotism of the Japanese-American soldiers is unbelievable!" Phil said with fervor.

"I read that the newspapers reported that for weeks our White troops were unsuccessful in rescuing the Lost Texans. Sounds like Tom's battalion had the willpower to rescue them, but they sure paid for it by losing so many men." I looked far off into the distance as the clouds began to build up.

"I'm glad at least our country honored those that were left. Have you heard from Sumi yet? Is she back?"

I didn't want to connect with Phil as my eyes drifted off past the canteen. "I got a very upsetting letter from her last week." I choked, "Her husband did volunteer for the Army and was one of the soldiers killed rescuing the lost battalion." I blinked several times, then I couldn't control myself any longer and cried into my hands.

Phil took out his handkerchief and gently patted my face. He put his arm around me as I buried myself into his shoulder. We had forgotten we were in a public place and separated as soon as we remembered.

"The depressing part is Sumi's still staying at Topaz, even though she can leave. She doesn't have the mental strength to move, being a widow with two young children."

"They're keeping the internment camps open?"

"I guess so."

"I'm sorry." Phil's compassionate gaze gave me comfort as he squeezed my hand.

The 442nd "Christmas Tree" Army regiment

Chapter 40: A Loss and a Celebration

Victory over Europe came and went, followed by the news of the two atomic blasts. We all knew it would only be a matter of time.

The heat of August made it hard to go to work. The yard gave off more of a humming noise instead of clanging and buzzing; I could sense there was something different in the air. I had an eerie feeling at the pit of my stomach because the yard was so still.

As I reached the entryway, a foreman guarded the stairs to the ship. He turned away every woman and said, "We don't need ya now, girls. Our boys are on the way back and ready to work. You can all go back to your kitchens!"

I eyed all the gals. We had the same hangdog look.

Roslyn cried with great sobs. "My husband ain't coming back. I'm a widow now. How am I gonna support my kids?"

No words were spoken as we shuffled off the Kaiser Shipyard property for the last time.

Phil spied me outside the yard and swung me around saying, "It's really over!"

My despondent feeling over the news of my job ending and Roslyn's troubles left me upon feeling Phil's cheer. I was ecstatic to share the celebration of the good news, the end of the war.

Phil was filled with enthusiasm. "My mother went to

190

visit her sister. Why don't you come over to the house?"

"I don't think so. Joe wrote me, he'll be home in a few days."

"Then it will be our last time, like I promised. I'll let you go when your husband comes back." He tried to lead me toward his car, but I stood solidly stuck to the pavement.

He ignored my stubborn stance, and opened the passenger door. "Come, sweetheart, one last time."

I reluctantly slipped into the seat.

"Let's drive to San Francisco first to see everyone celebrating the end of the war."

"I'd love that! I'm glad it's over, but I'll miss my job and all the friends I had."

We rolled our windows down and enjoyed the warm breezes of the summer floating in and out.

"I got a letter from Tom, probably my last one. It was written a few months ago," Phil said as we rode down the highway.

"I wondered if his battalion was involved in the final part of the war." I stretched out my arm and moved my fingers through the wind.

"As a matter of fact, the 442nd helped liberate people from the concentration camps in Dachau."

"Really! It must have been frightening to see a concentration camp."

"It's ironic to me that when he returned to the states he was released with his family from their own camps."

"My God, that's a twist of fate. Thank goodness it's all over. I hope this will be the war to end all wars."

191

Phil nodded in agreement, turning onto Market Street. "So do I."

All the traffic came to a halt. Phil turned the engine off as a wave of white flowed down the avenue—sailors galore! We stuck our heads out the window, listened to all the hoorays, the explosive noises of the horns, fire sirens, and plant whistles. All the kissing and hugging was a glorious sight. Women and children rode on the shoulders of many of the soldiers. People threw their hats in the air and caught them. Almost everyone had a bottle of beer in their hands while standing in the middle of the street.

Caught up in the excitement, Phil leaned over and we embraced, both feeling a sense of relief and happiness all combined into one.

As we approached Phil's neighborhood, we watched children somersaulting. Mothers banged pots with lids and people rode bicycles every which way. All the church bells rang and seemed to say, "The war is over! The war is over!"

Phil's house was cozy and neat, like a new store's showroom, as one would expect living with a mother who stayed home all day with no children.

He grabbed and kissed me with hunger in the middle of the living room. I stepped away from him.

Feeling my uncertainness, Phil said, "Lolly, I love you so much, but I'll keep my promise, this will be the last time."

I returned his embrace, time feeling like hours. An aching slowly crept upon me as he kissed me into the bedroom. Our lovemaking was an intensity of fire, knowing the affair would have to end.

Chapter 41: Back to the Kitchen

Meeting Joe at the train station was awkward for the children, as they hadn't seen their father in quite a long time. My cross and my wedding band had been put away for nearly two years and felt cold on my skin. Joe rushed off the train through the crowds of soldiers and hugged me tightly. I tried not to stiffen. Then he hauled up both the children as they shyly leaned back toward me.

Within days Joe got his old job back from the trucking company. After work, he would gruffly greet us and light up his cigarette. It was just like old times again, I glumly thought. With his recent raise he bought a brand new Motorola radio that fit neatly on a table in front of his rocker. It blared out:

"At the Ford Plant in Michigan, women are carrying placards that read: 'Stop discrimination because of sex and how come no work for women?'

Ladies, the shipyard gold rush is over!"

From the kitchen I heard Joe jeer, "Dames belong at home with their husbands. How dare these girls want to take away jobs from our boys who just returned from the war? Don't they get it? Men are the breadwinners; women are the homemakers."

I didn't have the strength to argue with him. Instead,

I thought miserably thought about the two widows I knew, Sumi and Roslyn, and wondered how they were getting by. After Joe went into the garage to fiddle around, I sat in the living room and read a letter from Diana.

Dear Sis:

I'm glad not be working anymore, I bet you are too. Edwin got a job in the city as a manager of a zinc company. We bought a three-bedroom house on Long Island with help from the VA bill. He'll take trains and subways to get to work because we know it is best to start a family in a safe neighborhood, not in a city. I'm get rounder and rounder every day and we have an adorable bassinet just waiting for our new precious package! Has Joe bought a television yet? It's all the rage. I love mine!

Write soon,
Love Sis

"I'm Dreaming of a White Christmas" played on the radio as I read a *Popeye* comic book to Billy. I skipped over the part that said, *Let's blast 'em Japanazis!* I read the last page, and showed him how the new "Gooey Gupp" Joe had bought him for Christmas could be flattened out on the comic. We peeled it off. Billy laughed with delight when Popeye and Olive Oyl magically appeared. Billy grabbed the Gooey Gupp, bouncing it on the floor and ceiling. I almost slapped his hand, but resisted as the memory of Mrs. Ginzberg's voice came into my mind: "Let the children be children."

Laughing, I said, "Give it to me, Billy."

He bounced it at me. I caught it and bounced it into the kitchen. Billy gleefully ran after it.

Edna came in holding her roller skates. "Mommy, can

you show me how to put them on?"

Joe, full of the Christmas spirit, said, "Come on outside with me, babycakes, I'll teach you how it's done."

Billy and I went out with them. Joe placed one of the skates on Edna's oxford shoe. He pushed the ends of the skate together and tightened it with a key, then put the other one on her other shoe. Edna weaved, tilted, then confidently glided along the sidewalk as we all clapped. Billy ran in and grabbed his new silver steel coil spring toy called a "Slinky." Joe showed him how it would slink down the front steps. I was lucky to find this Christmas toy, as it was very well advertised in the newspaper and hard to find. The article said the idea for the invention originated with an engineer who watched a coil spring fall from the deck of a naval ship.

I left Joe outside with the children and read the *Ladies Home Journal,* enjoying the alone time.

What Men Want

Men want the women of their dreams in the kitchen. Girls, if you want to be a doctor or a lawyer—marry one! Pursue a "Mrs. Degree" or a Ph.T, Putting Hubby Through. Girls, you can't have a career and be good housewives at the same time. There are plenty of activities for you to keep busy while your husband works or until the children are older. Join a club from your church, PTA, or any Scout group. This will preserve your marriage.

After Christmas vacation, Edna came home from the Richmond Public Grammar School waving a letter at me. I read it out loud:

We are asking all mothers to help their children fold cranes to send to Japan. Origami is the Japanese art of folding squares of colored paper into tiny shapes.

Our class has read the story of Sadako Sasaki, a Japanese girl who survived the atomic blast of Hiroshima. After the war, the bomb poisoned her with a disease called leukemia. At age 11, Sadako folded Japanese paper cranes while in the hospital because she believed in the ancient Japanese legend that by folding 1,000 cranes you will be granted one wish. Sadako Sasaki had a wish for world peace.

Sadako died at age 12, after folding 644 paper cranes. A sculpture was built for her. The monument showed Sadako on top of a mountain with her arms raised high, a crane in her hand. This prayer was engraved upon the stone:

This is our cry

This is our prayer

Peace on Earth

Please make as many cranes as you can with your child to send to school, and we will mail them to Japan where thousands of Origami cranes from all over the world are being sent. Our class has been doing a unit on peace after such a devastating war.

Together we studied the diagram from the teacher and folded many cranes together. I reflected on the war. How could so much death and destruction motivate people to accomplish such feats of cooperation and productivity? I was able to help build an entire ship in four days. Holding my tiny gold cross, I wondered…why couldn't peace become the motivating force to bring this country together, instead of war?

I waddled out to get the mail as Fala followed behind. He watched me closely as I reached inside the box. Sumi was on my mind, yet I hoped not to hear from her.

I knew I couldn't continue corresponding with her, or visit her even if she did end up nearby. Peace in my family was now top priority, especially since there was a new addition on the way. I could only hope that the baby had blue eyes like all of us… and not brown like Phil's.

A familiar Model A drove by very slowly. I fastened the mailbox lid and quickly turned back toward the house. Fala's fine, pointed ears pricked up as I hummed a line of a song running through my head, "A sigh is just a sigh…"

History of the Japanese-American Internment

1/14/42: Presidential proclamation required all aliens to report any change of address, employment, or name to the FBI. Enemy aliens were not allowed to enter restricted areas. Violators of these regulations were subject to arrest, detention, and internment for the duration of the war.

Executive Order 9066, 2/21/42: Authorized the Secretary of War to prescribe military areas (the entire West Coast and Southern Arizona) from which any or all persons were to be excluded to protect against espionage and sabotage.

Military commanders enforced compliance. The Secretary of War was authorized to provide for the residents of military areas: transportation, food, clothing, shelter, use of land, shelter supplies, equipment, utilities, facilities, medical aid, hospitalization, and other services as necessary. The Federal Bureau of Investigation would investigate alleged acts of sabotage.

Public Proclamation No. 1, 3/2/42: Anyone having "enemy" ancestry had to file a change of residence notice if they moved.

Executive Order 9095, 3/11/42: Created the Office of the Alien Property Custodian, which had authority over all alien property interests. All assets were frozen.

3/24/42 Public Proclamation No. 3: Declared a curfew (6:00 a.m. 8:00 p.m.) for all enemy aliens and persons of Japanese ancestry within the military areas.

5/3/42: Civilian Exclusion Order No. 34: General DeWitt ordered all people of Japanese ancestry, whether citizens or noncitizens in Military Area No. 1 (West Coast), to report to "assembly centers" where they would live until moved to permanent "Relocation Centers."

Between 110,000-120,000 people of Japanese ancestry were subject to this mass relocation program, two-thirds of whom were U.S. citizens.

Eighteen Temporary Civilian Assembly Centers were used to house the Nisei (Japanese-Americans) and Issei (Japanese citizens living in the USA): racetracks, stables, migrant workers' camps, Civilian Conservation Corps camps, county fairgrounds, and warehouses. They were located in California, Arizona, Washington, and Oregon.

Permanent Internment Camps built: Ten in Arizona, Colorado, Wyoming, Arkansas, California, Idaho, and Utah.

Justice Department detention camps: There were eight that held German and Italian detainees in addition to Japanese Nisei and Issei. They were located in Texas, North Dakota, Montana, New Mexico, and Idaho.

Citizen Isolation Centers for problem inmates: There were three located in Arizona, Utah, and New Mexico.

Federal Bureau of Prisons for detainees convicted of crimes: There were three camps located in Arizona, Kansas and Washington.

United States Army Facilities held German, Italian, Issei, and Nisei detainees. There were eighteen located in California, Florida, Louisiana, New Mexico, Wisconsin, Arizona, Maryland, Oklahoma, and Hawaii.

There were 11,507 people of German ancestry and 10,000 people of Italian ancestry who were interned and evacuated from the military areas.

Only Hawaiians of heightened perceived risk (1,200-1,800 Japanese ancestry) were interned.

Many internees were temporarily released from their camps to harvest crops due to the wartime shortage of labor.

National Student Council Relocation Program: students of college age were permitted to leave the camps (2,263) to attend institutions willing to accept students of Japanese ancestry.

There were Japanese-Americans who remained in their own homes and were not evacuated if they were living in the Midwest, East, or South.

Statement of United States Citizen of Japanese Ancestry (loyalty questionnaire) 1/23/43: No. 27 and No. 28 were the most controversial.

- **No. 27:** Are you willing to serve in the Armed Forces of the United States on combat duty wherever ordered?
- **No. 28:** Will you swear unqualified allegiance to the United States of America and faithfully defend the United States from any or all attack by foreign or domestic forces, and forswear any form of allegiance or to the Japanese emperor, to any other foreign power or organization?

Percentage of people who answered question #28 of the loyalty questionnaire positively: 89.4.

Number of internees who answered negatively to question #28: 5,589. They renounced their U.S. citizenship and were sent to the Tule Lake High-Security Segregation Internment Camp.

The Tanforan Temporary Assembly Center in San Bruno, California, 4/42-10/42 had 7,800 Bay Area people of Japanese descent.

California State Historic Landmark #934 Tanforan Racetrack Japanese Assembly Center, Tanforan Park Shopping Center on El Camino Real, San Bruno reads: "Racetrack opened in 1899 and had racing seasons until it burned down in 1964. Many famous horses raced and won here. In 1942, Tanforan became a temporary assembly center for over 4,000 persons of Japanese ancestry who were to be interned for the duration of World War II."

Topaz Permanent Internment Camp, Millard County, Utah, 140 miles south of Salt Lake City, 19,800 acres. Peak population: 8,130, 9/11/42-10/31/45. Temperatures: 106 degrees in summer to -30 degrees in winter, frequent dust storms from constant wind.

James Hatsuki Wakasa walked near the internment fence, did not hear the sentry's warning, and was shot to death on 4/11/43.

Toyosaburo Fred Korematsu: 1/30/19-3/30/05, born in Oakland, California. Lost his job at Kaiser Shipyard after the bombing of Pearl Harbor because of his ancestry. When Executive Order 9066 was issued, he became a fugitive, changed his name on his identification card and was arrested for evading internment (breaking Public Law 503, enemy alien staying in a military area) and put in jail. While incarcerated, an attorney from the American Civil Liberties Union filed a lawsuit challenging Executive Order 9066. The attorney bailed him out, but Mr. Korematsu was arrested and taken to Tanforan assembly internment camp. The case Korematsu v. United States Supreme Court claimed the detainment of loyal citizens was unconstitutional. It lost on 12/18/44 on the grounds that the compulsory exclusion was justified because of emergency and the military necessity to curtail the civil liberties of a specific racial group.

On 1/19/83, two attorneys brought Korematsu's case before the federal court in San Francisco, and the U.S. District Court formally vacated Korematsu's conviction. Korematsu said, "I would like to see the government admit that they were wrong and do something about it so this will never happen again to any American citizen of any race, creed, or color. If anyone should do any pardoning, I should be the one pardoning the government for what they did to the Japanese-American people."(1)

1/2/45: (Eight months before the end of the war) all internees were given $25.00 and a train ticket back to their former homes if they wanted to return.

Mine Okubo: 6/27/12-2/10/01: received her Master's of Fine Arts from U.C. Berkeley before she was interned at the Tanforan and Topaz internment camps. She had a realistic, creative, as well as humorous mind. Okubo documented life in an internment camp and wrote the book *Citizen 13660* published in 1946 by the University of Washington Press. Cameras and photographs were not permitted in the camps, so she recorded everything in sketches, drawings, and paintings.

American Japanese Claims Act of 1948: To receive compensation for property losses, internees had to show proof. The IRS destroyed most of the 1939-42 tax records, and many were unable to establish their claims as valid. Japanese-Americans filed 26,568 claims totaling $148 million in requests; $37 million was approved and disbursed.

Nothing was paid for internment time or for loss of earnings or profits.

Senate Bill 1009, 8/10/88: Restitution and apology. Payments of $20,000 went to each individual interned. A public education fund was sent up to help ensure that this would not happen again. Eighty-two thousand Japanese-Americans received an apology and monetary redress.

Civil Liberties Act of 1988: Signed into law by President Reagan that the incarceration was a fundamental and grave injustice. "For these fundamental violations of the basic civil liberties and constitutional rights of these individuals of Japanese ancestry, the Congress apologizes on behalf of the Nation."

The fishing community on Terminal Island in San Pedro Bay, California, was evacuated and never re-established.

In 1952 Issei could become citizens.

References:
Alonso, Karen. *Korematsu v. United States*, Enslow Publishers, Springfield, N.J. 1998.

Burton, Jeffrey F.; Farrell, Mary M.; Lord, Florence B.; Lord, Richard W. *Confinement and Ethnicity: An Overview of World War II*, Chapter 3.

Chin, Steven A., Ed. Alex Haley. *When Justice Failed: The Fred Korematsu Story.* Steck-Vaughn Co., New York, NY. 1993.

Densho oral history website: "Densho: The Japanese-American Legacy Project," Director, Tom Ikeda. Free digital archive containing hundreds of video oral histories, photographs and documents. Http://www.densho.org.

Executive order 9066, (President Franklin D. Roosevelt, Doc. 42-1563; Filed, 2/21/42; 12:51 p.m.)

Hill, Kimi Kodai, ed. *Topaz Moon: Chiura Obata's Art of the Internment.* Berkeley: Heyday Books, 2000.

Inada, Lawson Fusao, ed. *Only What We Could Carry.* Berkeley: Heyday Books, 2000.

Japanese-American National Museum: Hirasaki National Resource Center
http://www.janm.org/nrc/accfact.php

Okubo, Mine, *Citizen 13660,* Seattle: University of Washington Press, 1994.

Uchida, Yoshiko. *Desert Exile.* University of Washington Press, 1982.
http://www.bookmice.net/darkchilde/japan/camp2.html
http://www.janm.org/projects/clac/topaz.htm
http://academic.udayton.edu/race/02rights/intern04.htm
http://www.tulelake.org/history.html
http://www.intimeandplace.org/Japanese%20interment/reading/loyaltyquestions.html

Korematsu v. U.S., 1944WL 42849, Appellate Brief.

Endnotes:
(1): Chin, Steven A., Ed. Alex Haley. *When Justice Failed: The Fred Korematsu Story.* Steck-Vaughn Co., New York, NY. 1993. Pg. 95.

History of Japanese-American Soldiers During WW II

_____   _____   _____

- 20,000 Japanese-American men and women served in the U.S. Army during WW II.
- 3,000 Hawaiian and 800 Japanese-American men were inducted into the 442nd Infantry Regiment.
- The 442nd Regimental Combat Team was the most decorated unit, for its size and length of service, in the entire history of the U.S. Military. They suffered the highest casualty rate and were known as the "Purple Heart Battalion." More than 700 men were killed. The 4,000 men who initially came in April 1943 had to be replaced nearly 3.5 times. In total, about 14,000 men served, ultimately earning 9,486 Purple Hearts and an unprecedented eight Presidential Unit Citations. Twenty-one of its members were awarded Medals of Honor. Members of the 442nd received a total of 18,143 awards. The Japanese-American soldiers' average height was 5'3" and average weight of 125 pounds.

References:

Asahina, Robert. *Just Americans: How Japanese-Americans Won a War at Home and Abroad.* Gotham Books, 2006.

Go For Broke! Madacy Music Group, Inc., Produced by Dore Schary, 1951. Realistic movie about the Japanese-American 442nd Regimental Combat Team.

Going For Broke DVD, documentary, distributed by Qestar, Inc. Hosted by Senator Daniel K. Inouye. http://www.sfmuseum.org/war/issei.html

Sadako Sasaki was two years old when the Hiroshima bomb dropped near her home. By age 11 she was diagnosed with leukemia, caused by radiation exposure from the atomic bomb. Sadako folded paper cranes in the hospital, according to the Japanese belief that if one folds 1,000 cranes they will be granted a wish. She was only able to fold 644 cranes. Her wish was for world peace. (Paper was very scarce at the time.) Sadako Sasaki died at age 12, October 25, 1955. In 1958 a memorial was built for her and all the children who had died from the effects of the atomic bomb. It is a statue of Sadako Sasaki holding a golden crane at the Hiroshima Peace Memorial, or Genbaku Dome. At the foot of the statue is a plaque that reads: "This is our cry. This is our prayer. Peace on Earth." Today, over nine metric tons of paper cranes are delivered to Hiroshima annually.

Corer, Eleanor. *Sadako and The Thousand Paper Cranes.* Published by Puffin, 1977.
www.wikipedia.org/wiki/SadakoSasaki

History of the Tuskegee Airmen

Yancy Williams, a Howard University student, sued the government to become an aviation cadet. As a result, the Army Air Force, in November, 1941, set up a pilot training center for Negroes at Alabama's Tuskegee Institute (TAAF).

From 1941-1946, 994 pilots graduated from TAAF; 450 served overseas for combat duty.

Tuskegee Airmen shot down 251 enemy planes and logged more than 15,000 sorties. None of the bombers they escorted were ever shot down.

The 332nd Fighter Group lost 66 men and had 33 taken as prisoners. Among the 850 awards the group won were 150 Distinguished Flying Crosses, eight Purple Hearts, 14 Bronze Stars, and 744 Air Medals. The 332nd was the only fighter group in the entire Army that did not lose a bomber from enemy attack.

Freeman Field Mutiny, 4/11/45: 162 arrests of black officers. Three were court-martialed, one convicted. **Lt. Roger Terry,** a Tuskegee airman, was court-martialed for jostling a White officer, was fined $150.00, reduced in rank, and dishonorably discharged in 11/45. He received a full pardon, restoration of rank, and a refund of his fine in 1995. The remaining officers received instructions for clearing their records.
The 477th was never deployed into combat.

Captain James Walker bailed out of his crippled fighter plane and landed in Belgrade. Seventeen-year-old **Aleksandr Zivkovic** found and hid him. Walker spent 39 days dodging Nazis with the help of the Serbs. Zivkovic immigrated to America in 1971 and reunited with Captain Walker. (1)

Benjamin O. Davis, Jr. became the first black Army Air Force general.

Executive Order 9981, 1948: signed by President Harry S. Truman, racially integrated the United States Armed Services.

Endnotes:
(1) New York Daily News March 31, 1999.

References:
Brooks, Phillip. *The Tuskegee Airmen*. Compass Point Books, Minneapolis, Minn. 2005.

Homan, Lynn M. & Reilly, Thomas. *Black Knights: The Story of The Tuskegee Airmen*. Pelican Publishing Co., Gretna, LA. 2001.
http:www.tuskegeeairmen.org/Tuskegee_Airmen_Hitory.html

Warren, Lt. Col. James C. *The Tuskegee Airmen Mutiny at Freeman Field*. The Conyers Publishing Company. 2001.
http://en.wikipedia.org/wiki/Freeman_Field_Mutiny
http://www.tuskegeeairmen.org/uploads/RogerTerry.pdf

History of Working Women During WW II

Throughout WW II, more than 210,000 women were permanently disabled in factory accidents, and 37,000 died. (1)

The average factory woman put in 48 hours over a six-day work week. (2)

Women ages 14-50 worked in factories during WW II. (3)

More women were working after WW II in 1947 than during the war; they were paid less for essential civilian work.

Most women were laid off from better paying industrial jobs after the war. (4)

Endnotes:
(1) Ralph Lewis, Brenda. "War Labor Board equal pay for equal work," 1942. Reader's Digest: *Women At War*. New York. 2002. p. 79.
(2) Weatherford, Doris. *American Women and World War II*. New York: Facts on File, 1900. p. 162.
(3) Ralph Lewis, Brenda, pg. 79.
(4) Mersky, Leder. *Thanks for the Memories*. London: Praeger, 2006. p. 94-95.

History of Shipbuilding in Richmond, California, During WW II

⬤▬▬ ▬▬⬤ ⬤▬▬

There were four Richmond shipyards that built 747 ships during WW II, employing more than 90,000 people.

Liberty Ships were built in 13 states by 15 companies in 18 shipyards. A total of 2,751 Liberty Ships were built. A Liberty Ship cost under $2,000,000, was 441 feet long and 56 feet wide. Her three-cylinder, reciprocating steam engine, fed by two oil-burning boilers, produced 2,000 hp and a speed of 11 knots. Her five holds could carry over 9,000 tons of cargo, plus airplanes, tanks, and locomotives lashed to its deck. It could carry 2,840 jeeps, 440 tanks, or 230 million rounds of rifle ammunition. A Liberty Ship could carry a crew of 44 and 12-25 Naval Armed Guards. It was slower and less strong than a Victory Ship. The *SS Robert E. Peary Liberty Ship* in Richmond held the record for being built in the shortest time, four days, 15 hours and 29 minutes after the keel was laid. This record has never been surpassed. She sailed on her maiden voyage ten days later on November 22, 1942, carrying 43 seamen and 17 naval personnel. Liberty Ships were named after prominent deceased Americans. Eighteen were named for outstanding African-Americans. Any group that raised $2 million in war bonds could suggest a name for a Liberty Ship. The founder of a 4-H group, the first Ukrainian immigrant to America, and an organizer for the International Ladies Garment Union all had a Liberty Ship named after them. *SS Jeremiah O'Brien Liberty Ship* was built in 1943, in So. Portland, Maine.

210

The ship is presently moored in San Francisco. Virtual walking tour: www.ssjeremiahobrien.org.

There were 531 **Victory Ships** built during WW II in six shipyards in the United States. They were larger and had greater horsepower engines than Liberty Ships. Victory Ships were 455 feet long, and had a speed of 15-17 knots. *SS Red Oak Victory Ship* was built in Kaiser Richmond Shipyard #1, and was launched on 11/9/44. It is the only surviving vessel of the 747 that were built. To tour the ship go to ssredoakvictory.org.

There were 90,000 workers at the Richmond shipyards at their peak, diminishing to less than 35,000 by 8/45. In 1945, shipbuilding in the yards was shut down. The shipyards were dismantled by 7/45. Many ships were sold for scrap. There were approximately 10,000 people out of work.

Richmond's population: 23,642 in 1940 to 130,00 by April 1943. (1)

Endnotes:
(1) *The Second Gold Rush: Oakland and the East Bay in World War II.* Johnson, Marilynn S., University of California Press, 1996. pg. 33.

References:
Marinship. Finnie, Richard. Taylor & Taylor, San Francisco. 1947.

Rosie the Riveter Web Site:
www.rosietheriveter.org/shiphist.htm.

History of Child Care in Richmond, California

Before the war, there were 7,000 children in Richmond. In September 1944 there were 35,000 children. (1)

At its peak, with 24,000 women on the Kaiser payroll, Richmond's citywide child facilities maintained a total daily attendance of 1,400 children. Thirty-five nursery schools were established in the Richmond area during WW II. (2)

The Lanham Act of 1941 provided Federal funding for day care. It helped construct schools and other facilities in areas experiencing heavy migration due to the growth of defense industries. It did have many shortcomings. Funds were not made available until well into the war. Day care during the war was never fully funded. (3)

Henry J. Kaiser (1882-1967) testified before Congress arguing that services for women, including child care facilities, were essential to improve the manpower situation and the government should finance them. (4) Kaiser directed the construction of Child Development Centers and sought advice from **Dr. Catherine Landreth (1899-1995)**, Doctor of Psychology, who wrote several books and articles about child development. Landreth was an innovative expert on enhancing child development in centers and how best they should be designed, interiorly as well as exteriorly. (5)

The Maritime Child Development Center was the first publicly funded center in the U.S. It was funded and constructed by the U.S. Maritime Commission. The center was heavily subsidized by Kaiser. (6) It had a total enrollment (not simultaneously) of 718 children in 1943-1944 with a capacity of 180 children per day. The center had a ratio of accredited teachers to children of one to six. (7)

A nurse, art instructor, music director, pediatrician, dental hygienist, psychiatrist, and librarian made the rounds of many centers in Richmond.

The centers did not serve many African-American children and black women were not part of the administration or staff. (8)

In July 1944, 3,000 nursery schools were established in the United States. (9)

Endnotes:
(1) nps.gov/pwro/NatRegPullmanChildDevCenter.pdf.
(2) *Growing Pains*, Kaiser newsletter "For'N'Aft," September 1944, 8.
(3) Rose, Elizabeth. *A Mother's Job*, Oxford Press, 1999. Pg. 166 .
(4) Greenbaum, Lucy, *As Kaiser Sees it*, *The New York Times*, 31 October 1943.
(5) Landreth, Catherine. *Education of the Young Child – A Nursery School Manuel*. John Wiley & Sons, Inc. N.Y. 1942.
(6) Brown, Hubert Wen. *The Impact of War Worker Migration on the Public School System of Richmond California, from 1940 to 1945*.
(7) Ph.D. Diss., Stanford University, 1973, pg. 269.
(8) Johnson, Marilynn S. *The Second Gold Rush, To Place Our Deeds: The African-American Community in Richmond, CA.*
(9) Moore, Shirley Ann Wilson, *To Place Our Deeds*, University of California Press, Berkeley, CA, 2000. Pg. 68.

Jeane Slone

References:
nps.gov/pwro/NatRegPullmanChildDevCenter.pdf
nps.gov/pwro/NatRegMaritimeChildDevCenter.pdf

History of the Port Chicago Explosion

On July 17, 1944, 320 men (of whom 202 were African-Americans) were instantly killed at the Port Chicago, California Naval base in Contra Costa County.

Port Chicago Mutiny 9/14/44: Fifty men refused to load munitions at Mare Island base after the Port Chicago explosion. The trial lasted six weeks. All fifty men were found guilty, sentenced to fifteen years in prison and a dishonorable discharge. Forty-seven of the fifty were released in 1/46; three served additional months in prison. Two remained in the prison's hospital recuperating from injuries; one seaman was not released because of bad conduct.

On 1/46 the Navy granted clemency to the sailors from the Port Chicago base; forty-seven were paroled to active duty.

The Navy asked Congress to give each victim's family $5,000. Representative John E. Rankin of Mississippi had it reduced to $2,000 when he learned most of the victims were black. (1) Congress settled on $3,000. "Of the 320 dead, only 51 could be identified." (2) The tombstones read "Unknown, US Navy, 17 July 1944." (3)

"In 1994, a review of the proceedings found that racism had played a role in the work at Port Chicago and in the subsequent mutiny proceedings." (4) In 1999, President Clinton officially pardoned **Fredrick Meeks,** one of the three surviving men who were tried in 1944, of any charges of mutiny." (5)

The Navy was desegregated in 6/45.
"The work done at Port Chicago was vital to the success of the war, yet the story of the men who carried out that work is often overlooked." (6)

The Port Chicago explosion accounted for 15% of all African-American deaths during WW II. (7)

Endnotes:

(1) Allen, Robert L. *The Port Chicago Mutiny*, Berkeley, CA. Heyday Books. 2006. P. 67. ISBN 9781597140287.
(2) http://www.history.navy.mil/faqs/faq80-4a.htm
(3) Bell, Christopher, and Elleman, Bruce, *Naval Mutinies of the Twentieth Century: An International Perspective.* Routledge. 2003.
(4) "Port Chicago—A Critical Link." National Park Service *Port Chicago Naval Magazine* National Memorial.
(5) Ibid.
(6) Ibid.
(7) Ibid.

To tour the Port Chicago, California Memorial site call 925-228-8860, web site: www.portchicagomemorial.org

Minority History During WW II

Over a half million African-Americans left the South in the forties to work for the war effort; 600,000 Black women were employed by the defense industry.

Forty-five thousand women, including 800 Native American women, served in the Armed Forces.

Twelve thousand Native American women left reservations for war jobs.

Half a million Mexican-Americans enlisted in the Armed Forces.

Over 145,000 women were in war production jobs. In 10/45 there were only 37,000 employed. By 1946 over three million women left the workforce.

References:

Colman, Penny. *Rosie The Riveter. Women Working on The Home Front in World War II.* Crown Publishers, N.Y. 1995.

Giles, Nell. *Punch In, Susie! A Woman's War Factory Diary.* Harper & Brothers Pub., N.Y. 1943.

Gluck, Sherna Berger. *Rosie The Riveter Revisited.* Penguin Pub., N.Y. 1987.

Hinamatsuri Japanese Doll Festival:

http://en.wikipedia.org/wiki/HinamatsuriKuriddm

Josephson, Judith Pinkerton. *Growing Up in World War II, 1941-1945.* Lerner Pub., Minneapolis. 2003.

Lewis, Edward V., O'Brien, and Robert O'Brien. *Ships.* Life Science Library. Time Inc., N.Y. 1965.

Litoff, Judy; Smith, David. *American Women in a World at War, Contemporary Accounts From World War II.* Scholarly Resources, Inc., Wilmington, Del. 1997.

Litoff, Judy; Smith, David. *Since You Went Away.* University of Kansas Press. 1991.

Moore, Christopher Paul. *Fighting For America, Black Soldiers-The Unsung Heroes of World War II.* Presidio Press, N.Y. 2006.

National Park Service, U.S. Department of the Interior. Rosie The Riveter/World War II Home Front National Historical Park.

Olian, Joanne. *Everyday Fashions of the Forties as Pictured in Sears Catalogs.* Dover Pub., N.Y. 1992.

Petersen, Christine. *Rosie the Riveter.* Scholastic Inc., N.Y. 2005.

Takaki, Ronald. *Double Victory, A Multicultural History of America in World War II.* Little, Brown & Co., N.Y. 2000.

Tateishi, John. *And Justice For All, An Oral History of the Japanese-American Detention Camps.* University of Washington Press, 1984.

Von Miklos, Josephine. *I Took a War Job.* Simon & Shuster, N.Y. 1943.

Wise, Nancy Baker, and Christy Wise. *A Mouthful of Rivets.* Kpsseu-Bass Inc., San Francisco, Ca. 1994.

Yellin, Emily. *Our Mothers' War, American Women at Home and at the Front During World War II.* Simon & Schuster, Inc., N.Y. 2004.

The American Girls Collection. *Welcome to Molly's World 1944, Growing up in World War Two America.* Pleasant Co. Publications, Middleton, WI. 1999.

Visit Richmond Museum of History, Richmond, CA:

http://wwwrichmondmuseumofhistory.org

Songs

As Time Goes By: Music/lyrics, Hupfield, 1931 Warner Bros. Music Corp. Movie, *Casablanca.* Sung by Dooley Wilson, 1942.

Boogie Woogie Bugle Boy: Composer: Don Raye, & Hughie Prince, 1/2/41, Warner Bros. Music Corp.

Chattanooga Choo-Choo: Composed by Mack Gordon & Harry Warren. Movie, *Sun Valley Serenade*, Glenn Miller Orchestra, RCA, Bluebird B-11230-B, 1941.

I'm Dreaming of a White Christmas: Composer: Irving Berlin, sung by Bing Crosby, 1942.

Mairzy Doats: Composed by Milton Drake, Al Hoffman, and Jerry Livingston. 1943.

Oklahoma: Composed by Richard Rodgers and Oscar Hammerstein II. 1943.

Pistol Packin' Mama: Composer, Al Dexter, 1942.

Rosie the Riveter: written by Redd Evans & John Jacob Loeb, Paramount Music Corporation, 1942.

Swinging on a Star: Composed by Jimmy Van Heusen. Lyrics by Johnny Van Heusen. Decca Records, 1944.

We're the Janes Who Make the Planes: Sidney Miller, Universal Music, 1944.

You Always Hurt the One You Love: recorded by the Mills Brothers, Decca Records, #18599. 1944. 20 weeks/best seller.

You Are My Sunshine: Peer International Corp., Composers: Jimmie Davis and Charles Mitchell, 1940. State song of Louisiana.

About the Author

starshotsphotography@gmail.com

Jeane Slone is the Vice President of the California Redwood Writer's Club, a member of the Healdsburg Literary Guild, Military Writer's Society of America, and the Pacific Coast Air Museum. She is also a tutor for the Library Legacy League.

Ms. Slone published the historical fiction *She Flew Bombers,* about the true adventures of the Women Airforce Service Pilots during WW II.

Jeane enjoys researching pieces of the forgotten past, especially involving female heroines and multi-cultures.

She is currently researching her third novel, *She Was a Spy During WW II.*

Ms. Slone is an avid kayaker, and paddles on the Russian River, which is outside her window.

Visit: wwwjeaneslone.com Email: info@jeaneslone.com

23412274R00132

Made in the USA
San Bernardino, CA
19 August 2015